Overnight Hercules for Network Security

Become a Security Analyst

Michail Tsikerdekis

Copyright © 2024 - Michail Tsikerdekis

All rights reserved.

Northshore Press – Bellingham, WA, 98226

https://northshorepress.co

No part of this publication may be reproduced, distributed, or transmitted in any form or by any means, including photocopying, recording, or other electronic or mechanical methods, without the prior written permission of the publisher, except as permitted by U.S. copyright law.

Notices

To the fullest extend of the law, neither the Publisher nor the authors assume any liability for any injury and/or damage to persons or property as a matter of products liability, negligence or otherwise, or from any use or operation of any methods, products, instructions, or ideas contained in the material herein.

ISBN: 9798339591726

Library of Congress: Application submitted

DEDICATION

To all the network security geeks out there that love experimenting and protecting our cyberspace.

CONTENTS

1	Introducing Network Security	1
2	Preparing to Secure your Network	17
3	Understanding the Basics of TCP/IP	45
4	Securing your Endpoint Devices	71
5	Evaluating the Perimeter	87
6	Detecting Data Theft using NetFlow	101
7	Harnessing Intrusion Detection Systems	115
8	Hunting for Malware	133
9	Recognizing Threats from Within	143
10	Working Remote or on the Cloud	155
11	Powering Up your Skills	167
12	Building Towards a Proactive Secure Future	173
13	Next Steps	183

1 INTRODUCING NETWORK SECURITY

- Why network security?
- How do we perform network security?
- Examining your laptop's network security.
- Viewing network connected processes on your laptop.

Overview

Welcome to the beginning of what is an exciting exploration of modern networks and security. If you have already picked up this book, you are likely interested in network security on a personal level for your own network, or perhaps you want to take this to the next level and become a security analyst. Regardless, I wrote this book with the hope of guiding you along the way.

This book provides everything I couldn't find in a single source when I taught my network security courses at the university. It's also critically different from others because it keeps theory to a minimum. I want you to learn things that are applicable instead of cluttering your head with too many terms (though there are still plenty of terms because cybersecurity). I also included some real-world examples from my personal experiences in the book, including incidents experienced by my students who have monitored real computer networks through the Public Infrastructure Security Cyber Education System (PISCES)(https://pisces-intl.org/).

If you have no prior experience with Information Technologies (IT), fear not, I also wrote this book with no prior knowledge required. Do you understand basic high school math? Then you should be good to go.

And no, I'll keep math to a minimum.

- High school math?
- Appetite for security?
- A laptop and other digital devices?
- A home network?

As for the format of each chapter, there is one important difference compared with other books out there: the book aims to teach you competence, not just skill. What this means is that in each chapter, I will describe the concepts that you need to universally apply to different problems. Then, in the companion repository (https://github.com/tsikerdekis/overnight-hercules-network-security), you will find specific instructions. For example, if I need to talk about creating and renaming files, I will describe the concept, and in the repository, you can find instructions on how to do that in various operating systems. This keeps the book current, and you can keep reading anywhere you are, even if you don't have your computer with you. Then, when you are ready, you can practice the concepts on a computer.

So, what is it that you will need for the first chapter? An appetite to sit back and let me try and answer the bigger question: why?

The big picture

Network security is important but why? This is what we will attempt to answer together first.

Let's start playing the devil's advocate. If our important (critical) data are in our computers and laptops, then shouldn't we pay attention to these? Well yeah, in a world of isolated islands, that would be a great idea.

In reality however, those islands are very much connected, and even worse (for security purposes), they exchange information with one another. As such, information can be easily stolen while it's being transported, much like a person stealing mail from the mailperson.

Then again, we can also use these connection points, to steal from one computer and then pivot to another. So, it's not only that we can steal what moves but also what sits in various computers since we can just move around the network.

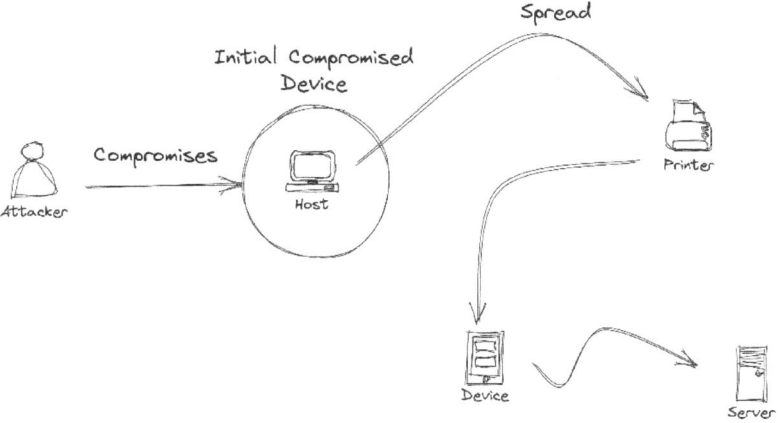

To make matters worse, this little network is also connected to the rest of the internet, where anyone can do the same.

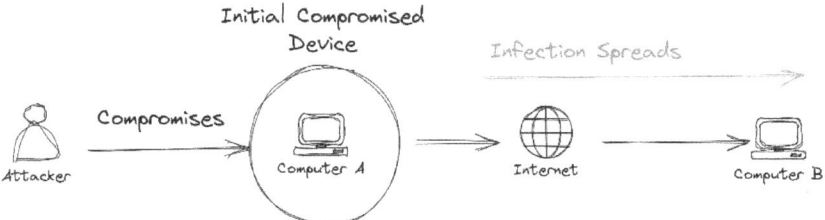

So, what we are left with is a realization that unless we start securing networks, data and our devices are not safe and just about anyone can exploit them.

The solution involved moving in this direction: first raising awareness and then generating security models. By "model" here, we simply mean ways of thinking about a problem or lenses for viewing a problem from different angles.

One such model is the *Confidentiality, Integrity, and Availability* (CIA) model.

Without going too much in depth, the idea is to examine how to secure a network or device by observing it through different lenses. For example, availability in a network context requires that data can freely flow 24/7 through a network line. Cutting the cable would pose a threat to availability, so we can focus on fixing that. Integrity focuses on preserving the data from being tampered with or accidentally modified by the system, whereas confidentiality requires that no person without authorization can access the data.

If the above sounds too abstract, then you are right. So, the powers that be generated several guidelines to ensure security in networks. These guidelines were incorporated into larger security frameworks. You can think of these as checklists.

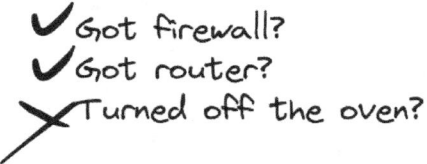

For example, a popular framework is the National Institute of Standards and Technology (NIST) Cybersecurity Framework (that's a mouthful). This includes step-by-step instructions to perform various tasks, including protecting against and responding to security threats. Another well-known framework is the NIST Special Publication 800-53, titled "Security and Privacy Controls for Federal Information Systems and Organizations." One of the checklist items from this framework is as follows:

Ensure that each user account on the network has a unique identifier (e.g., username, user ID) and is associated with only one individual.

Notice that it does not tell us how we can check this "box," but rather what the "box" that needs to be checked is. This is the first challenge with cybersecurity. There are many ways that we can secure networks, and not all of them are effective. Context can also play a role in this; securing a chicken coop is probably easier than securing a hospital, but don't quote me on that.

Before long, in tandem with frameworks, legislators recognized the importance of security and established various regulations. Among the most notable are compliance regulations, which, as the name implies, mandate organizations' compliance. This can be burdensome for affected entities. Examples of compliance regulations include the Health Insurance Portability and Accountability Act (HIPAA) in the U.S., applicable to medical facilities; the Payment Card Industry Data Security Standard (PCI DSS), which pertains to entities handling credit card transactions; and the General Data Protection Regulation (GDPR), a data protection and privacy regulation applicable to the European Union. These regulations include a lot of elements for network security along with general security, such as physical (e.g., putting a titanium door for a vault). There are a lot more regulations. Here's some in an exaggerated Venn diagram in terms of how they overlap:

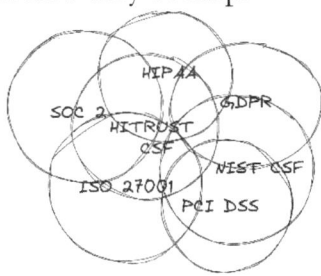

At this point, you may start asking, "Well, I thought I was going to do some cool stuff, not learn about laws." Well, you would be right, but these regulations have actually changed attitudes regarding network security. In fact, most of these require organizations to secure and monitor their networks. That's to say that there is a need for people to do security.

So, who handles security? Anyone who interacts with a digital device. Well, ideally. There are some specific roles, but given the rapid changes in the field, it's not uncommon to see a utility manager also doubling as a security administrator. This is actually a true story. However, some more common roles include:
- System or network administrator
- Cloud engineer
- Security engineer
- Information security analyst
- Compliance officer
- Security consultant
- Chief Information Security Officer

Now, not all of these roles are directly involved in network security, but elements of what they do require them to have an understanding of network security. Another thing is that these are just labels. For most security professionals, there are many hats that they wear to make things happen. There is also a difference between the entry requirements for these jobs. System administrators and security analysts tend to be entry-level positions in the industry. That is also why the focus of this book is on security analysis.

- Security Analyst - Entry-Level
- Security Administrator - Entry-Level to Intermediate
- Incident Responder - Entry-Level to Advanced
- SOC Analyst - Entry-Level to Advanced
- Compliance Analyst – Intermediate to Advanced
- Cybersecurity Specialist - Intermediate
- Security Auditor – Intermediate to Advanced
- Digital Forensics Analyst - Intermediate to Advanced
- Security Trainer/Educator - Intermediate to Advanced

So, let's talk about Information Security Analysts (the term used by the U.S. Bureau of Labor Statistics). At the time of this writing, the median salary is $112,000, and the job outlook over the new decade is expected to be 32% growth. This is high compared to other occupations, by the way. And just to ensure that this is not a fad, in 2014, the job was listed with a median salary of $86,170 and an expected growth of 37%. In fact, the growth projection was slightly off. At the time, they listed 75,000 professionals, while currently, there are 168,000 for this occupation. That's roughly 120% growth over a decade.

Still with me? So, what education is required to become a security analyst? Often, a Bachelor of Science is what is reported alongside statistics; however, a quick look at the current positions for security analysts (June 2024) on Indeed.com reveals 226 open positions requiring just a high school diploma and another 534 requiring an associate degree. Of course, I would be remiss if I didn't mention that positions requiring a Bachelor's or Master's degree number around 2,200 each. But looking back at the question posed, the answer is High School. My goal is not to minimize the importance of university education; after all, as a professor, I'm the biggest advocate for all the advanced knowledge that you can gain through a university. However, if you are looking for a first step, then with a bit of experience gained through experimentation, you may have a shot at work as a security analyst. In confidential conversations with industry hiring professionals, it's clear that while credentials certainly play a role (especially in determining salary), what truly matters during the hiring process is what you have demonstrated. In fact, it's not uncommon to hear questions such as, "Tell us about your own home network," during hiring interviews. Another goal of this book is to provide you with enough information so that, hopefully, you can have something elaborate to say in response to this question.

Understanding network security

Let's take the first step in securing your network. Why your network? Because it's there; you can see it, you can touch it, and more importantly, it holds all your data and other devices. To secure your network (and your data), there is a process that is followed, which goes something like this:

1. Identify all *assets* (i.e., data and equipment of value).
2. Rank the importance of each asset based on the *impact* that it would have on you if it were to be lost or damaged.
3. Identify potential threats out there in terms of how serious they are. For your home network you can probably exclude government-sponsored hackers.
4. Rank the *likelihood* that all these threats (collectively) will carry out a successful attack in some way (i.e., *attack vector*) against your assets.
5. Multiply impact with likelihood to determine the *risk*.
6. Sort the list of assets based on the calculated risk and start securing as many devices as you can as far as your budget can take you.

The above is the happy-meal version of the process that most organizations will use to secure their assets. In fact, the formula about risk is often summarized as:

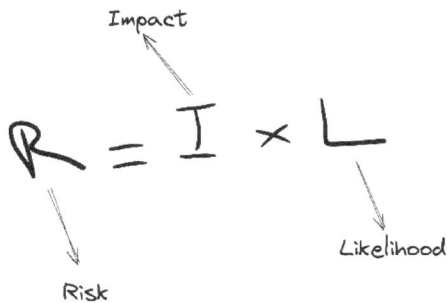

You may be asking, "Well, how do I rank impact and likelihood?" You can use any kind of scale. There isn't really a formal scale used, but if you are looking for one that is used most frequently, it is the low, medium, high scale. Based on that, the risk assessment table would look like this:

Likelihood

	Low	Medium	High
Low	Low	Low	Medium
Medium	Low	Medium	High
High	Medium	High	High

Impact

Let's try to apply this to your network. Grab a piece of paper and identify assets, likelihood, and impact. You can even doodle threat actors, just for fun, like I did below.

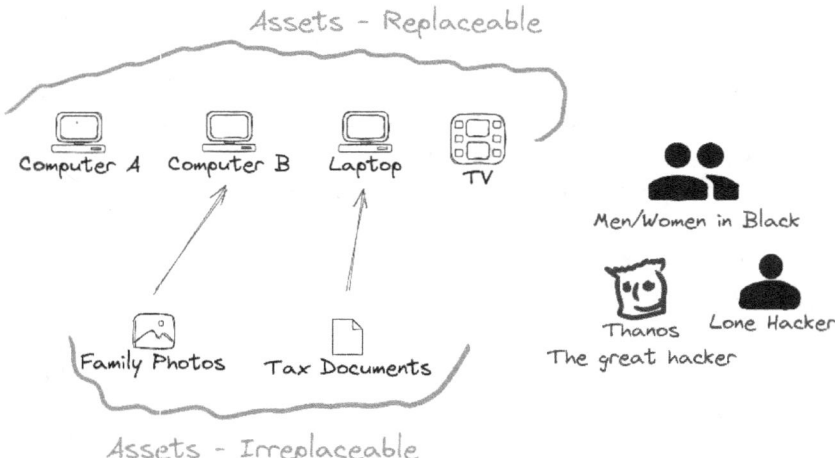

Notice that my list includes anything that connects to my network, whether it is wirelessly (which includes Bluetooth) or through a wire. Technically, some of my important data lives in the cloud (i.e., someone else's computer) to which you have limited control over their network security. We can ignore that for now since it is covered in a later chapter. For now, look at the top asset. I'm going out on a limb to say that it is your laptop. It holds data that is critical and not easily replaceable. Cost-wise, it is also an asset that is more expensive than others. In terms of threats, you can estimate that most attackers are just random people that want to make money off your data, but still, some of these may be sophisticated. So, then, you have to ask, how likely is a compromise to this device? For that, you have to draw from your knowledge (albeit at the moment limited) of all the possible nasty ways that attackers can ruin your laptop's day. Here's a short list:

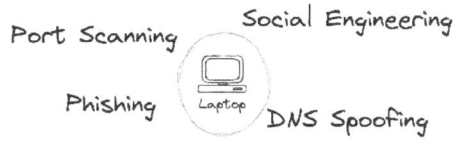

Yes, the world of networks is a dangerous place. Next, you can also determine the likelihood that these attacks will succeed. Here's a fun secret: If you possess no prior security experience, you can put that likelihood down as "high." Why? You don't know what you don't know, and you know only what you do. Confused? What I'm trying to say is to start at the worst case; it's safe to do so since you can survive being afraid of a bear that is not really in the bushes than if the bear truly is. So, the risk for your laptop is currently:

$$R = I \times L = High \times High = Super\ High$$

Starting with "high" is a great place to get us to ask questions. We lower the likelihood by applying *controls* to an asset and/or network. For example, email spam is bad, and many people fall victim to it. After all, it is a game of statistics; the more they receive spam, the more likely they are to click on one. Have you done your homework to read on what spam is, what the common patterns used in spam are, and kept up with the news on recent spam campaigns? Depending on how many of these you answered positively, you can start lowering the likelihood of a successful attack via email spam on your laptop. Organizations apply such controls in a more formal manner, such as employee safety training.

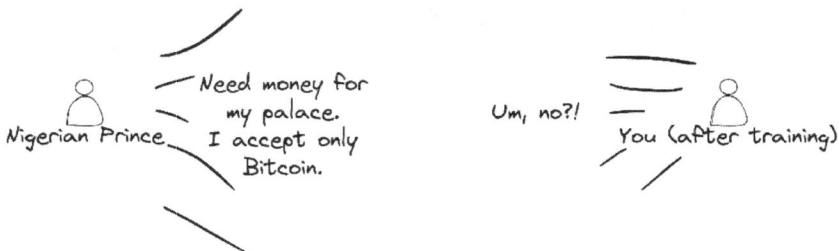

If you apply an additional control such as automated spam filters, you can reduce the likelihood of this attack to "low." This, in turn, changes the risk on your device ever so slightly.

$$R = I \times L = \text{High} \times \text{Low} = \text{Medium}$$

If you keep addressing most other common attacks on your laptop, you can eventually reach a point where the risk is lower than what you started with. Would that be the lowest of lows? Well, in security, that's not always possible. The goal is to lower it as much as we can, hope for the best, and should something bad happen, respond to it. That's where detection, analysis, and response come into play, and we discuss these in future chapters.

This is the process of securing networks in a nutshell. Just iterate until you can get to a satisfactory point.

Making your first network security actions

Let's start with the first steps by applying controls to your laptop. These include:

- Installing an antivirus (a cliché security talking point at this point).
- Configuring your laptop's firewall or at least making sure it is on.
- Checking which processes (software) on your laptop are listening for incoming connections from the network.

Antivirus

The first step is easy. Get an antivirus or make sure that at least your default system's antivirus is active. What does antivirus have to do with network security? It can prevent your computer from getting infected from internet activity (e.g., browsing websites) or it can prevent your computer from infecting others. A win-win at the cost of a bit more computational performance. If you are a hardcore gamer, you probably know what I mean.

Before we talk about antivirus however, we need to understand the first portion of software that sits at the beginning of your computer's memory: the *operating system*.

An operating system is software that translates instructions from other software to the hardware. You need to send a printing job to the printer through Word? Well, the operating system needs to translate that printing job into the language that the printer speaks. To achieve that, the operating system has a bunch of drivers. There are many parts to an operating system but all you need to know for now is that there is a *kernel*, the core part of the operating system, and everything else (i.e., your computer programs).

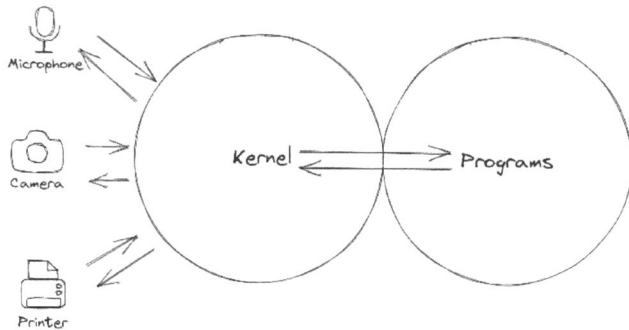

Operating System Ecosystem

What you can see above is a program talking to the kernel so that, in turn, they can communicate with a device and vice versa. Everything goes through the kernel, which also makes it the most critical part of your computer. The kernel is also the entity that holds the keys to the kingdom. If a program needs to do something that is considered privileged, then the kernel will have to determine whether that program (or the user that runs the program) is authorized to do it.

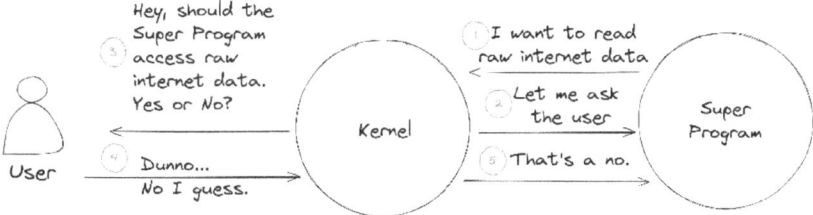

Anytime higher privileges are being requested from a program, the kernel will usually prompt the user. To be more specific, it would ask the *superuser*. Other names for this user are *administrator* and *root*. On your laptop, you are likely also the administrator, so the kernel will likely ask you to authorize such actions through a prompt. On Windows, this comes as an ominous cryptic message along the lines of "Do you want to allow this app to make changes to your device?"

What does this have to do with antivirus software? Well, an antivirus needs to perform a variety of privileged actions on your system, requiring *administrative privileges* (i.e., administrator authorization) to be granted to it upon installation. These privileges also make it significantly more challenging for a simple virus to disable the antivirus, as the virus would also need to acquire those privileges. Assuming the user does not authorize a program they do not trust, this scenario is unlikely to occur.

So, you need to make sure that an antivirus is installed and that it is up-to-date and receives frequent updates. Most antivirus software provides you with an easy way to verify this through a menu that looks like this.

Computer firewall

Firewalls work in similar ways to antiviruses (more in-depth discussion about them in Chapter 5). Default firewalls in systems ask the kernel for privileges to do advanced functions such as blocking traffic coming in from your Ethernet or Wi-Fi card (the hardware that connects you to the network). A firewall's function is two-fold: protect against what's coming in and protect against what's going out.

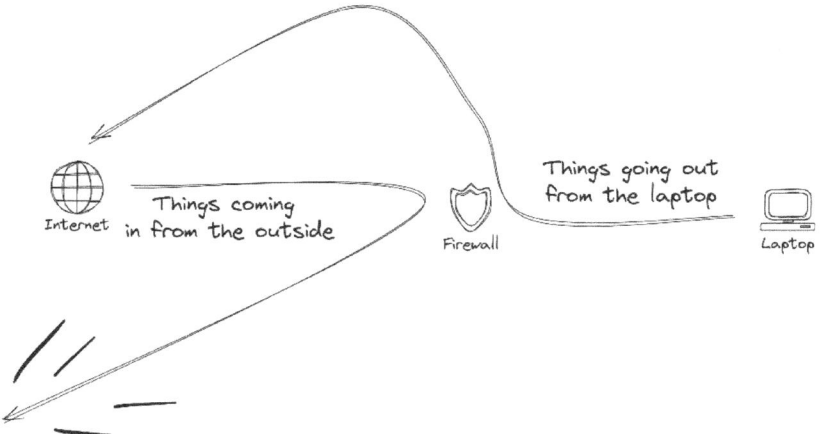

However, most firewalls on computers are more concerned with blocking incoming threats than regulating what goes out. Depending on your level of acceptable risk that you can tolerate, you can set your firewall to operate at the "paranoid" level. However, for the purposes of this step, you will need to verify that you meet the reasonable minimum requirements.

- You have a firewall that is enabled on your laptop.
- The firewall blocks all incoming connections unless otherwise authorized.
- The firewall allows all outgoing connections.

By connections above we mean directions of data. Incoming connections are data coming to our laptop and outgoing are data that our laptop sends to the world.

It is easy to verify whether your firewall is enabled by accessing the relevant security menu on your computer. This usually looks like this:

You may be wondering what the domain, private, and public networks are. These are simply zones. For now, you can think of them as whether you connect through Wi-Fi or via cable. You can specify different rules when using different zones. In this case, as long as your firewall is on everywhere, that's good enough.

The next step is to check whether incoming connections are blocked, and while we're at it, we can also verify whether outgoing connections are allowed. Most firewalls provide you with a way to do this. For example:

✗ Inbound connections that do not match a rule are blocked.
✓ Outbound connections that do not match a rule are allowed.

Once you verify the settings you also have the option to check for the rules, which basically say which programs are allowed to listen to incoming (inbound) or outgoing (outbound) connections.

Inbound Rules

✓ Xbox
  Zoom Video Meeting
✓ Windows Operator messages
✗ Skype

In most firewalls, there is a distinction between what is explicitly allowed (indicated by the checkmark in the above image), what is explicitly not allowed (Skype in the above image), and what is determined by the default rule. In this case, Zoom is blocked because, even though it is not explicitly mentioned, the default firewall rule is to block non-matched rules for inbound connections. However, it's worth noting that Zoom can still send data out; it just cannot receive them.

Listening processes

Next up, let's check what software is listening for incoming connections. It is the case that sometimes, even when you have not explicitly authorized it, different software can add or override firewall rules (e.g., software with administrative privileges or kernel software critical to the operating system functions). Network security is also about completing an inventory and verifying that things are working the way they should. There are command-line tools like netstat that can tell you which processes are currently listening for (open to) incoming connections. For example, the following command (using Command Prompt or Terminal depending on your operating system) can show you some of that information:

```
netstat -anob
```

This returns a list of various content, but you need to look for the lines that include the word LISTENING, like so:

```
Active Connections
```

```
 Proto   Local Address          Foreign Address        State
  TCP    0.0.0.0:135            0.0.0.0:0              LISTENING
 RpcSs
[svchost.exe]
  TCP    0.0.0.0:17500          0.0.0.0:0              LISTENING
22552
[Dropbox.exe]
```

This is a small example, but you can quickly see that on this computer Dropbox (a cloud backup software) accepts incoming connections. The actual list is a lot longer than the one presented here, and early on you may run into things that you haven't seen before. One of the skills that you need to develop is information seeking. For example, if you are not familiar with svchost.exe, you can either google "Is svchost.exe malicious?" or even pose the question to a generative language model such as ChatGPT. Here's the response from ChatGPT:

"Svchost.exe" is not inherently malicious; it's a legitimate system process in Windows operating systems. However, it's worth noting that malware sometimes disguises itself by using the same filename. This is a common tactic used by malware to hide its presence on a system.

At this point, I should note that searching the web for suspicious things that may or may not be malicious on your network is a lot like searching for medical advice on WebMD. It takes time and skill to progressively get better at it, and early on, everything will look malicious. So, be patient, persist, and let's explore the world of network security. When you're ready, explore the exercise presented in the online repository (https://github.com/tsikerdekis/overnight-hercules-network-security) that can better assist you in cementing what was discussed in this chapter.

2 PREPARING TO SECURE YOUR NETWORK

- Evaluate the available network technologies and devices.
- Configure your network devices, especially your edge router.
- Set up network security monitoring in your network and take the first steps toward security analysis.

Overview

Preparing to secure your network can be an overwhelming task, especially when done for the first time, as you have no clue what needs securing. Likely, you have completed the first task by establishing what your assets are and evaluating their risk. Regardless of your list, for most networks, there are some standardized steps that you are expected to take, especially in respect to your network devices and securing the network. In other words, while the execution may differ, the course of action is the same.

That is, security as a practice typically involves the following actions.

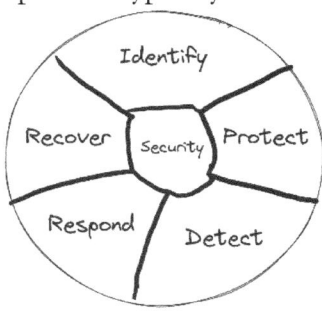

Likely, you have already conducted an inventory of assets and their associated risks in Chapter 1. You will continue this task by expanding the inventory list of network technologies associated with your network and then moving into the process of protecting them by evaluating their configuration profiles. Finally, you will also lay the groundwork for detecting threats in your network. Like before, don't forget to check the companion repository for further live exercises and instructions.

A final note before we start: There is a lot of network discussion in the chapter that I tried to keep relevant to security. Computer networks are taught in a full-length book, so condensing this information into a chapter means that some of the technical but security-irrelevant parts were left out.

Evaluating network technologies in networks

To secure network devices, you first have to understand the associated network technologies that make networks work. As such, identifying the types of technologies you have in your network is the first task.

Most of our modern internet infrastructure consists of a few key devices that enable communication to happen. These are:

- Modems
- Routers
- Switches

You'd be surprised to know that it's highly likely you have all three of them in your home. Do you have a device that was provided by your *Internet Service Provider* (ISP) so you can connect to the internet? Then, I'm willing to bet there's an 80% chance it makes use of all three technologies described above. In fact, we often refer to these devices provided by the ISP as either a modem or router (incorrectly, because they are often more than just one thing).

Modems

So, what are they and what do they do? Let's start with modems. *Modems* are devices that convert digital signals from your computer into signals that can be transmitted over telephone or cable lines, allowing you to connect to the internet.

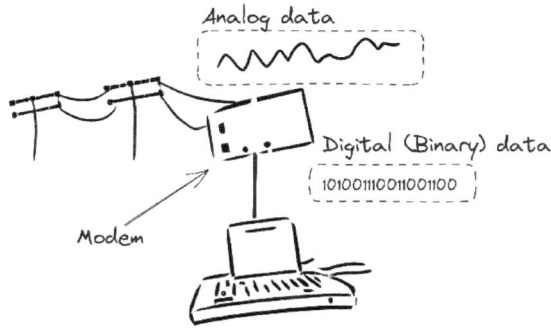

In the olden days, you would use a modem that plugged in to your telephone line and then to your computer (all wired). This had security implications that were missed by many unfortunate victims. The intuitive way to understand the security implications is if you consider the following: if you were to observe a space launch, would you prefer to be up close or (way) further back? Same for our computers. It's not a good idea to put them in the frontlines.

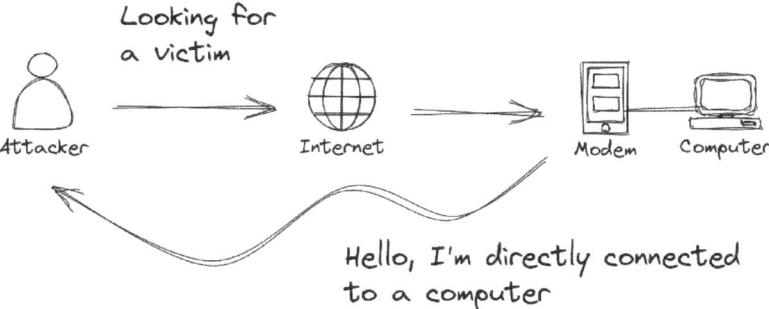

Routers

Routers followed as network devices although not for security purposes. Rather, *routers* are devices that help direct internet traffic between different devices in a network, like computers, laptops, and tablets.

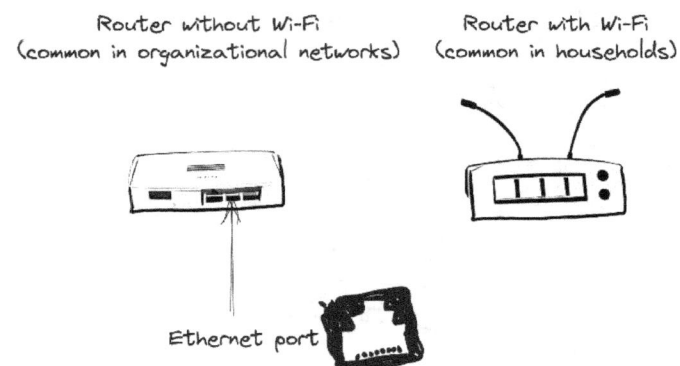

It's the name, the router of internet packets. Put many of them (but really) in a system and eventually, you can make up the whole internet infrastructure full of these devices that direct internet packets from one side of the globe to the other. This was achieved through the invention of the *Internet Protocol* (IP). This was a set of rigid instructions that dictate how a router should move a packet through a network. It is similar to mail delivery. Each letter contains instructions about the sender and destination, and each mail person handling the letter follows a set of rigid instructions (i.e., a protocol).

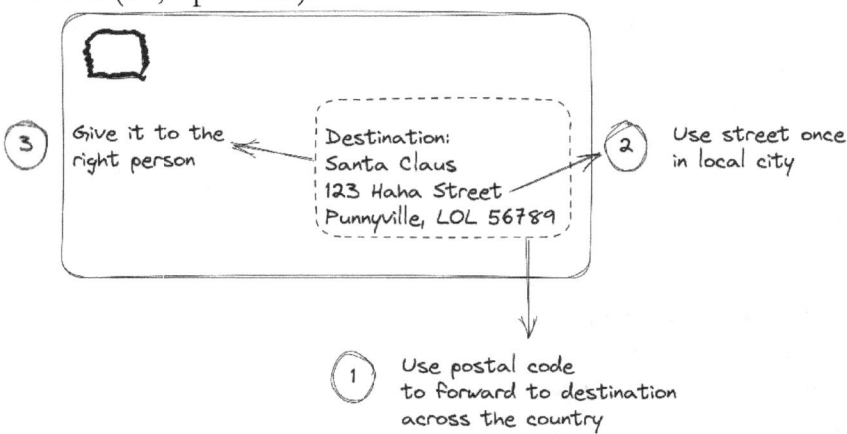

Most people refer to this process as the IP protocol, which is a redundancy if you think about it (you wouldn't say I ate pizza pizza).

But what goes through the "head" of a router when it receives an internet packet to figure out where to send it next? The size of the internet required a way to identify computers. We could number them incrementally (1, 2, 3, ...), but that would be too easy. Instead, we numbered them on the basis of four numbers between 1 to 255 separated by dots (e.g., 192.168.0.1). Why 255 and not 999 as the max? Well, computers operate on the basis of *bits* which can be 1 or 0. A collection of eight of these makes up a *byte*, which is the most basic building block for data in computers.

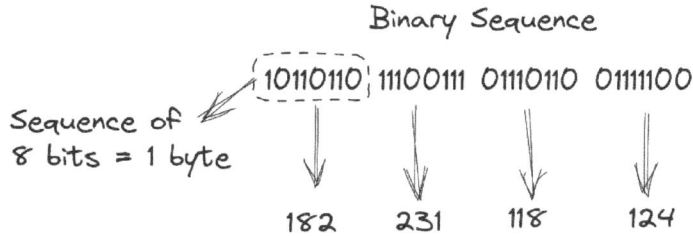

Four bytes represented as numbers

For example, a byte typically represents the letter "a", while a different byte can represent the letter "A". The range of available combinations between 1s and 0s in a byte allows us to represent whole numbers from 0 to 255. And so, we can arbitrarily assign letters to these numbers, but we can also use these numbers to, say, represent IP addresses. To make matters slightly more complicated, the IP addresses shown here are referred to as IPv4. "v4" stands for version 4. There is also a longer version called IPv6, because with so many computers online, we ran out of IPv4 addresses. Yes, all roughly 4 billion of them (256 values to the power of 4 slots if you are looking for the exact number).

Anyway, the key takeaway from all of this is that each computer on the internet gets an IP address, and routers use this as a means for moving data toward the destination. Just like a mail person, most routers have a list of rules on where to forward a packet depending on the IP address.

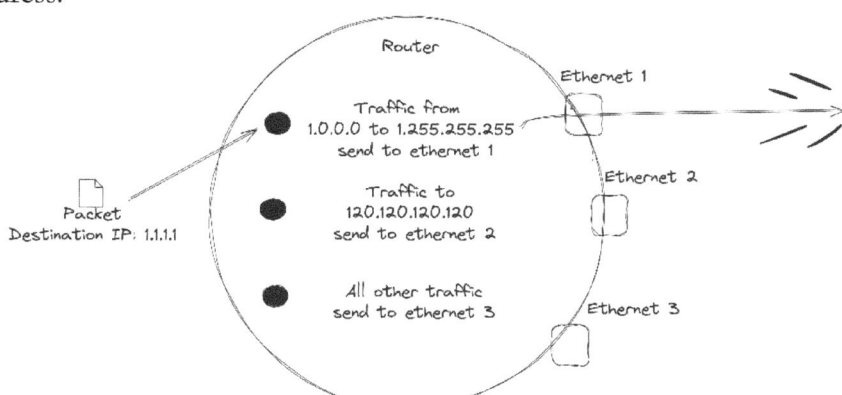

At the core of the internet (i.e., large telecommunications providers), these router lists are updated automatically as other routers come online or go offline. Additionally, each internet packet is not only accompanied by IP sender and destination address information but also other metadata defined at the beginning of the packet. This area is called the header, and it includes metadata such as the length of the transmitted packet.

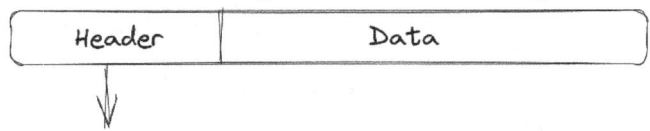

Source IP: 192.168.0.1
Destination IP: 192.168.0.2
Packet Length: 11
...

The thing to understand about IP and routers is that they are regulated by the *Internet Corporation for Assigned Names and Numbers* (ICANN). If you are a large telecom provider, you can request to receive a set of IP addresses. For organizational purposes, these are not assigned randomly but rather as a logical set. For example, one may receive addresses from 17.116.147.0 to 17.116.147.255 (a total of 255 addresses since only the last byte varies). Because writing ranges like these is tiresome, people use a shorthand notation for the range, such as 17.116.147.0/24. The "24" here means that 24 bits (or 8 + 8 + 8) are fixed. There are a total of 32 bits in an IPv4 address (4 x 8 bits), so the "24" indicates that only 8 bits are allowed to vary (0 to 255 possible combinations). These ranges are also referred to as *subnets*. Common subnets include /8, /16, and /24. However, it's worth mentioning that any other fixed number of bits can serve as an acceptable (albeit frustrating for engineers) subnet.

192.168.0.0/24 ⟶ 192.168.0.1 to 192.168.0.255

192.168.1.0/24 ⟶ 192.168.1.1 to 192.168.1.255

10.0.0.0/8 ⟶ 10.0.0.0 to 10.255.255.255

One final thing to know about subnets: If you are a big fish in the sea of the internet, you can request many subnets. It doesn't matter if sharing is caring; you can accumulate as many as you need. For example, many companies have numerous of these, and since it can quickly become an organizational nightmare to track who has what, we use the term "*autonomous system*" to describe a network organization that owns a lot of these. Typically, these are large telecom providers, but other companies can own IP addresses, such as Apple. Its autonomous system is AS714 (guess what "AS" stands for).

I can see a question from you: "Can I get a subnet?" Well, yes and no. You can acquire a subnet for a few thousand dollars through a broker and some waiting (yes, there are waitlists). But for most of us, we can get by just fine without needing to buy subnets. For one, your ISP provides you with an IP address so that the rest of the internet can deliver packets to you. Even more importantly, your internal home network already uses one of the reserved private subnets. They are referred to as RFC 1918 addresses, named after the document released by the *Internet Engineering Task Force* (IETF) that defined them. For IPv4, here's the list.

        10.0.0.0 to 10.255.255.255 (10.0.0.0/8 prefix)
        172.16.0.0 to 172.31.255.255 (172.16.0.0/12 prefix)
        192.168.0.0 to 192.168.255.255 (192.168.0.0/16 prefix)

That means that your home network and your friend's home network may be using the same subnet. We are all connected! However, your internet facing IP address at the outer side of your modem is different and so the packets can always find their right destination.

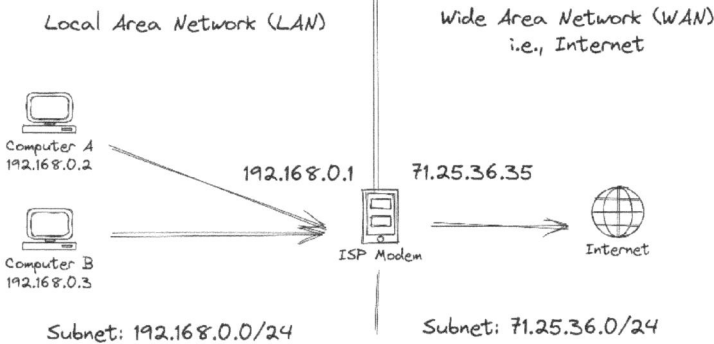

Switches

Switches are devices that connect multiple devices in a local network, such as computers or printers, allowing them to communicate with each other. The bolding of the word "local" was intentional. While a router's concern is about moving a packet in the right direction on the web of internet routers, a switch is concerned with getting a packet to its destination device. So, if your TV needs to access your phone's photos to display them, a local network transfer is likely happening (no internet involved), and thus a switch takes action. A switch is also a device that can be uniquely identified, often visually. It's the device that, for example, has many Ethernet ports.

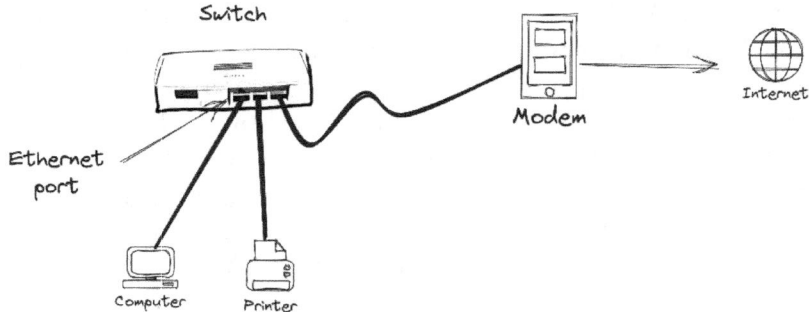

Yes, switches may look like routers, but functionally they are different. The switch makes decisions on what the final destination of a packet is and sends it there. You may be asking, "What about wireless?" Yes, switching action is also happening there in your local network; you just cannot see the ports as they are wireless. (That's a joke, by the way.)

Switches come with many bells and whistles as well. There are switches that are *web-managed*, meaning that you can access them through your browser and configure settings on them. Additionally, there are switches that allow for duplicating internet traffic from one port to another (*port mirroring*). This is the equivalent of tapping on a phone line and eavesdropping, and it has security ramifications that we will discuss later in this section.

A final point about switching is that it is ubiquitous. For example, the device provided by your ISP for accessing the internet is a switch, modem, and router.

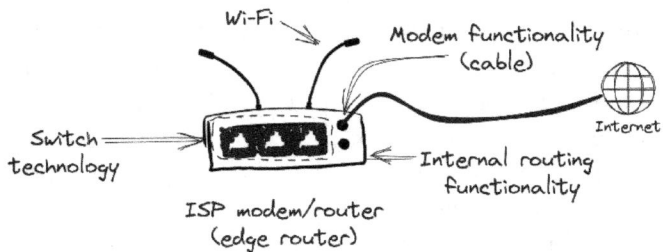

Switches also exist outside of your local network. They take the form of switching technology that is incorporated into internet routers. Switching, as an action, is considered to exist in a separate layer from routing. Think of a layer as a perspective when observing network actions. Referred to as Layer 2 (or the Data Link Layer), switching is concerned with hop-to-hop (device-to-device) communications. On the other hand, routing is part of Layer 3 (or the Internet Layer) where end-to-end communications are the focus.

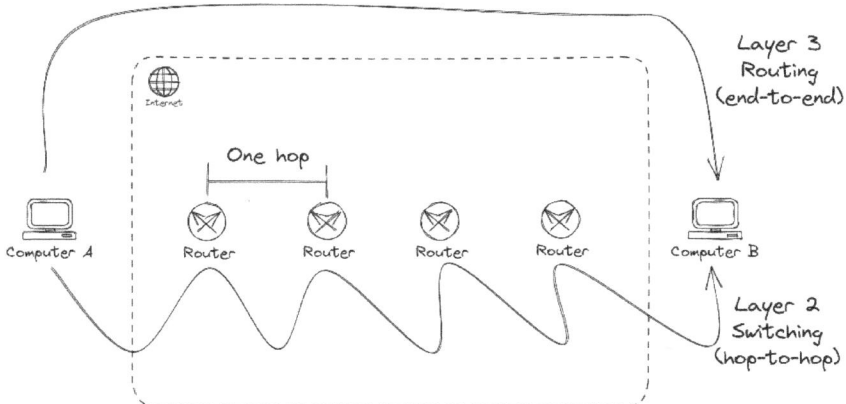

The packet still passes through each router; however, the router knows the final destination and simply forwards the packet toward it by determining the next device in the right direction.

Pinging the other side of the internet

Now that you understand how these technologies come together, it is time to perform your first network action: pinging. Although diagnostic, pinging another computer on the internet also has security ramifications. It can tell us that something is there and responding or that our firewall works, and as long as it's not abused, the activity is fairly benign.

Most operating systems come packaged with a ping tool that can be accessed via the Terminal or Command Prompt. The question is, what are you supposed to ping? Well, a common diagnostic for networks is to ping the default network's domain name service (DNS) relay server. We talk about this more in a later chapter, so all you need to know about this is that when you type a domain name (e.g., github.com) in your browser, a DNS server across the internet is involved. If your computer cannot reach the DNS server, then you have all sorts of problems. To ping Google's DNS server, you can type the following:

```
ping 8.8.8.8
```

Depending on your operating system, the command will continue pinging until interrupted using (Ctrl + C), or it will stop after 3 attempts. The output will look something like this:

```
Pinging 8.8.8.8 with 32 bytes of data:
```

```
Reply from 8.8.8.8: bytes=32 time=18ms TTL=58
Reply from 8.8.8.8: bytes=32 time=17ms TTL=58
Reply from 8.8.8.8: bytes=32 time=18ms TTL=58
Reply from 8.8.8.8: bytes=32 time=19ms TTL=58
Ping statistics for 8.8.8.8:
    Packets: Sent = 4, Received = 4, Lost = 0 (0% loss),
Approximate round trip times in milli-seconds:
    Minimum = 17ms, Maximum = 19ms, Average = 18ms
```

Zero percent loss is always a good sign, and low latency (especially <20ms) is great. In other words, we've sent a total of 4 packets out toward 8.8.8.8 (without knowing where it is), and somehow routers along the way pushed them to the right destination. Your modem was also involved since you are probably connected to the Internet through either cable or DSL (telephone lines). As for switching, it occurred at every step of the way, since once a router determines when to send the packet next, it uses switching technology to figure out the local network address of the next router. Notice that the path is not always what we would consider straight, as the Internet map does not correspond to geographic maps (i.e., there are all sorts of red tape on how and why a packet must travel).

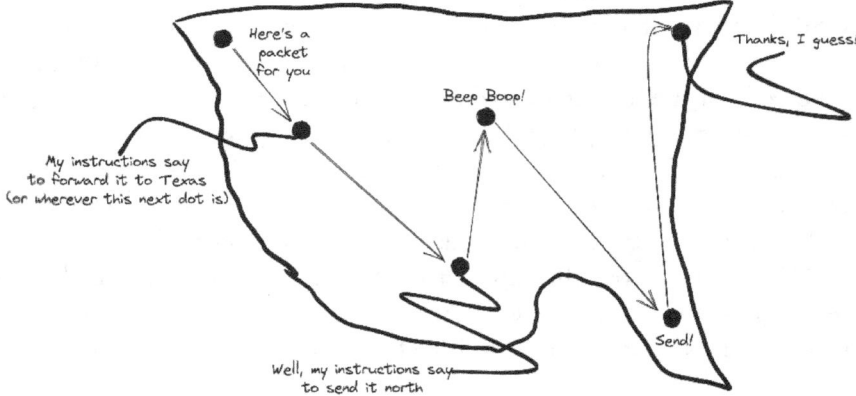

By the way, the address used for switching is not the same as the IP address; instead, it is called a *Medium Access Control* (MAC) address, which is hard-coded in all network devices (e.g., Ethernet card, wireless card, etc.). Windows calls it a "Physical Address," and an example of this is 30-24-32-BE-6A-09. The hyphens are for readability purposes, and each one of the two alphanumeric characters represents a byte in hexadecimal form (i.e., 16 characters, 0 to 9 and A to F). It's just more compact for reading than numbers from 0 to 255.

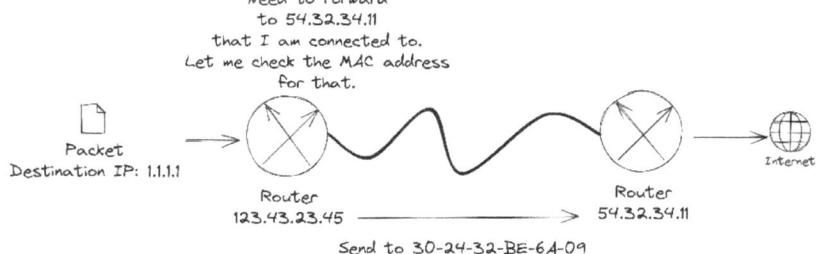

Anyway, the latest figure has little to do with security and very much to do with networking. Then again, it's pretty cool so why not get that networking perspective while also learning about security.

Examining network devices and their security configuration

Time to start evaluating the critical links in your network. Since the ISP's modem (also acting as a router and possibly a switch) is at the edge of the network (where all the action happens), it would be good to check that first. It's easy to identify the device since it's the core part of your network (i.e., without it, you have no internet). All modem/routers (hereafter referred to as *edge routers* for readability) have a web interface through which you can access further settings. You can access that interface through your browser as long as you can determine the modem/router's IP address:

- Figure out your network's subnet (i.e., the range of IP addresses in your local network).
- Determine your gateway.
- In all likelihood the gateway's address is that of your edge router.

To determine your network's subnet, you need to open up your laptop's Terminal or Command Prompt (you will need to do so with administrative privileges). Then type `ifconfig` (for Linux or Mac) or `ipconfig` (for Windows). The output will resemble something like this:

```
Windows IP Configuration

Ethernet adapter Ethernet:

   Media State . . . . . . . . . . . : Media disconnected
```

```
Connection-specific DNS Suffix  . :

Wireless LAN adapter Wi-Fi:


   Connection-specific DNS Suffix  . :
   IPv4 Address. . . . . . . . . . . : 192.168.0.31
   Subnet Mask . . . . . . . . . . . : 255.255.255.0
   Default Gateway . . . . . . . . . : 192.168.0.1
```

What do we see in the above output? Well, there are two network adapters (i.e., cards) on the computer: one for Ethernet and one for Wi-Fi. The Ethernet cable is not connected, while the wireless is connected, as indicated by the IP address assigned to the machine. You may be wondering, where is the subnet and what is the subnet mask? Well, in this example, the subnet mask indicates that the first 3 bytes are fixed. Basically, in binary, the portion that is fixed is represented with 1s.

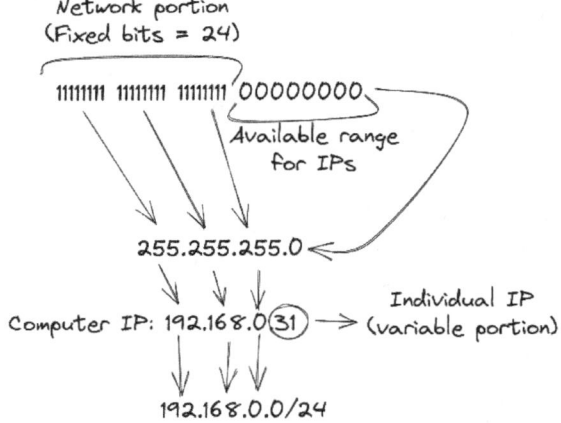

So, the subnet is a /24 (very common for home networks). Because the IP address of the computer is 192.168.0.31, we can extrapolate that the subnet is 192.168.0.0/24. In other words, the first 3 portions of the IP are fixed, and the last one varies. The 'Default Gateway' (sometimes also referred to as just 'Gateway') is 192.168.0.1. This is basically your router and your main way in and out of your local network. Why not 192.168.0.0? Well, the 0 address is reserved, so 1 is typically used for the router. The alternative is 254 (e.g., 192.168.0.254). Why 254 and not 255, which is the last number in the IP range? 255 is also reserved; more on that in Chapter 3.

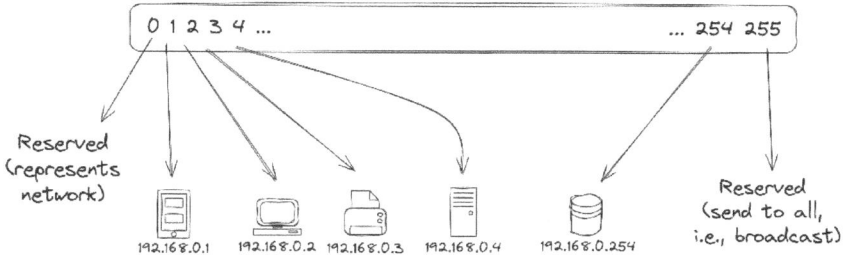

Other common local network subnets include 10.0.0.0/24 and 192.168.1.0/24. However, over the years, I've encountered even stranger configurations. For instance, one organization once utilized a Chinese subnet within their internal network. Now, that's confusing.

Alright, now that you know our IP address, and more importantly, the router's, you can type it into your browser:

http://192.168.0.1

The highly observant and paranoid reader will note at this point that I wrote "http" instead of "https" (i.e., the secure version for a router). You can also use "https://192.168.0.1", and it will likely work with most modem/routers, although your browser will complain about being unable to verify the modem/router's certificate. What you need to know for now is that "https" is better than "http" since the connection is encrypted. However, if your modem/router does not offer an "https" option, "http" is your only other choice. You just have to trust that nobody is eavesdropping on your local network. There's a 98% chance that you are safe. Besides, if they are eavesdropping, tracking you configuring your router is the least of your problems.

Enough with the scare tactics. Connecting to your router will likely greet you with a page requiring you to enter a username and password. Quite anticlimactic, isn't it?

Welcome to the gateway of possibilities!

You can typically find the credentials on your router's back sticker. Just lift your router, toss it in the air, and look for which side contains the sticker as it drops towards the ground.

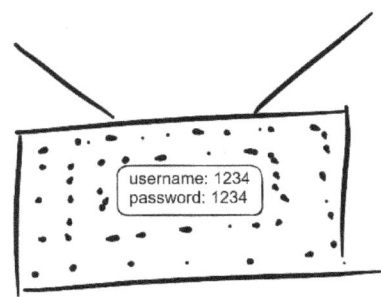

That was a joke, by the way. Once you find the credentials, enter them on the page. If all goes well, you should be able to access the configuration menu. These can vary, but by navigating through the various menus (often as part of a sidebar or top bar), you should be able to find the following critical options:

- Local IP Configuration (LAN)
- Wi-Fi
- Firewall
- Devices (Connected Devices)
- Port Forwarding
- Remote Management
- DMZ
- Device Discovery (UPnP)

Most of the menus and names may vary depending on the device manufacturer, and some examples are provided in the companion repository. However, the guidelines provided below are mostly the same across devices.

Local IP Configuration

In this menu, you will typically find the router's address (which sometimes can be changed), the subnet (or subnet mask), and the beginning and end of the IP address range. Confused? Well, it is true that the subnet will define the total range, but the router typically runs a dynamic IP allocation protocol called *Dynamic Host Configuration Protocol* (DHCP), and you can specify the available IPs that it should give away. For example, you could specify that anything from 192.168.0.2 to 192.168.0.100 is to be given to any device in need of an IP (after all, every device needs one), but then from 192.168.0.101 to 192.168.0.254, you can assign manually through the local device configuration (e.g., on Windows, you can specify the IP that the device should always use). As a good security practice, you may want to allocate fewer IPs dynamically and reserve some to be used manually on devices. This is what this menu typically looks like.

Gateway Address:	192.168.0.1
Subnet Mask:	255.255.255.0
DHCP Beginning Address:	192.168.0.7
DHCP Ending Address:	192.168.0.100
DHCPv4 Lease Time:	2 days

Wi-Fi

The Wi-Fi configuration typically divides itself between 2.4GHz and 5GHz. The former trades range for speed while the latter trades speed for range. Either way, the configuration for both is more or less the same.

Network Name (SSID):	DropItLikeItsHotspot
Mode:	802.11 a/n/ac
Security Mode:	WPA2-PSK
Channel:	157
Network Password:	TickleMyRouter
Broadcast Network Name (SSID):	Yes

You need to provide a network name, also known as SSID, that is descriptive enough to be identifiable but does not contain any critical or otherwise personal information. Modes can vary, but without going into depth, look for the protocol that includes the most dashes, e.g., 802.11 a/n/ac. This primarily affects speed. For security mode, you definitely should not use WEP or WPA, and instead use at least WPA2-PSK or WPA3. WPA2 requires a password for someone to connect to the wireless network, whereas WPA3 encrypts connections in such a way that if one is compromised, the rest are safe (WPA2 cannot guarantee that). Wi-Fi passwords are typically written and have a default password on the sticker (the same place where you find your admin credentials). You need to change that to something else.

How do you pick a password? Imagine a really strong password. Now, add a number and then a special character. Write it down, crumple the paper into a ball, and throw it in the garbage. Time and time again, people have proven that they are bad at picking passwords and make predictable choices—choices that an AI can guess. Don't believe it? Here's a ChatGPT dialogue:

Me: I was asked to come up with some secure password. So I came up with dragons. But I was asked to add a number. where should I put the number?

ChatGPT:

- *Append or prepend the number:* "dragons123" or "123dragons".
- *Insert the number in the middle:* "dra5gons" or "drag2ons".
- *Replace a letter with a number:* "dr4gons" or "drag0ns".
- *Repeat the number:* "123dragons123" or "dragons999".

If I were to add a special character like an exclamation mark, can you guess where it would typically be placed? If ChatGPT can come up with these answers, then any software can. Instead, you need to either work around this tendency to create simple, memorable passwords or obtain a truly random one. For example, one popular password manager website with a generator provided me with the following: `v82.4GH)E9?Q`. Choices between usability and security persist in network security, so I will refrain from being dictatorial about your choice but establish an acceptable risk and decide how strong your password should be. If you ever forget it, you can always log in to your router and find out what it is.

A final security setting under Wi-Fi refers to Broadcasting the Network Name. This setting is misleading. Disabling the broadcasting of SSID will cause your Wi-Fi network not to appear in the lists of computers. However, for Wi-Fi to function properly, special packets called beacons are sent out into the air, containing the SSID. Computers are simply instructed not to list them in their Wi-Fi lists. So, as far as settings go, this one impacts usability without providing any actual security benefits. A sophisticated attacker can still find your network's SSID.

Connected Devices

A router, by nature, needs to track the devices connected to it. This has nothing to do with the routing capabilities but more with the fact that modem/routers tend to perform a lot more functions than just routing (and modeming?) nowadays. Anyway, the list of connected devices tells you what was recently seen (but not in real-time) by your router, as well as how a device is connected and whether it has received an IP dynamically or statically (or reserved).

Host Name	DHCP/Reserved IP	Connection	
TYY_WWR	Reserved IP	Ethernet	Edit
Archer C9999	DHCP	Ethernet	Edit
ab:84:f3:fa:bc:89	DHCP	Ethernet	Edit
dc:a7:32:c8:ba:11	Reserved IP	Ethernet	Edit

In the image above, you can see several devices, some have a host name identified, making it easier to know what they are but others are identified based on the MAC address (the hard-coded value in their network cards). What's extra fun about the image above is that all of these devices are said to be connected through Ethernet but that is misleading. See, I have in my case a Wi-Fi router that then connects via ethernet to my modem/router.

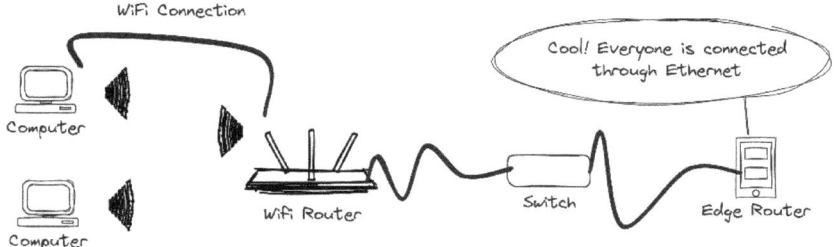

This way, even Wi-Fi devices appear to be Ethernet-connected to the edge router. So, an important security rule to remember: things are not always what they seem.

On to more important things. Anything designated as Dynamic (or DHCP) is allocated some IP on lease time. That IP, however, changes, so today's 192.168.0.2 for your laptop is tomorrow's 192.168.0.100. You can increase your lease's time, but at some point, it will change. That's okay for a bunch of random devices that you don't care about, but for assets that you deemed highly important, a fixed (i.e., static) IP address is preferable. After all, your router has one, so wouldn't it be nice to know that at least your laptop has one too?

So, how do you give it a static IP address? Well, assuming you have configured your DHCP (Local IP Configuration) to provide dynamically only a subset of the total available IPs, anything outside the dynamic range can be given to devices as static IPs.

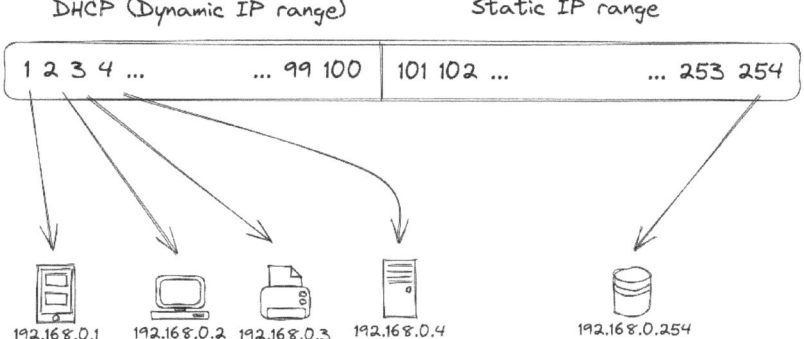

You can configure it on the actual device (e.g., computer's Windows network settings); however, many routers support the ability to assign a static IP through their configuration to a device with a specific MAC address. Since MAC addresses are unique and hard-coded on devices, this is a convenient way to assign static IP addresses.

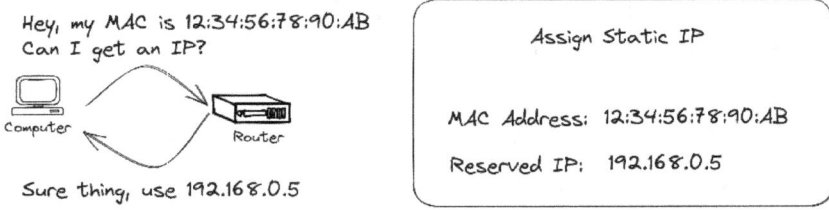

Most routers will allow you to directly edit and turn a dynamically allocated device into a static one right from their menu. Others may require you to provide the MAC address and IP address manually through a different menu. In that case, you will need to find your laptop's MAC address. I am showing you this in the companion repository since it varies for different operating systems.

After you have finished configuring your laptop, a disconnection and reconnection are more than enough to update its IP address. You can use the commands that you learned above (`ipconfig` or `ifconfig`) to verify that your laptop has acquired the new IP address.

As a final step, evaluate the rest of the devices on your network and consider assigning static IPs to the most critical ones. You can also do this in a pattern.

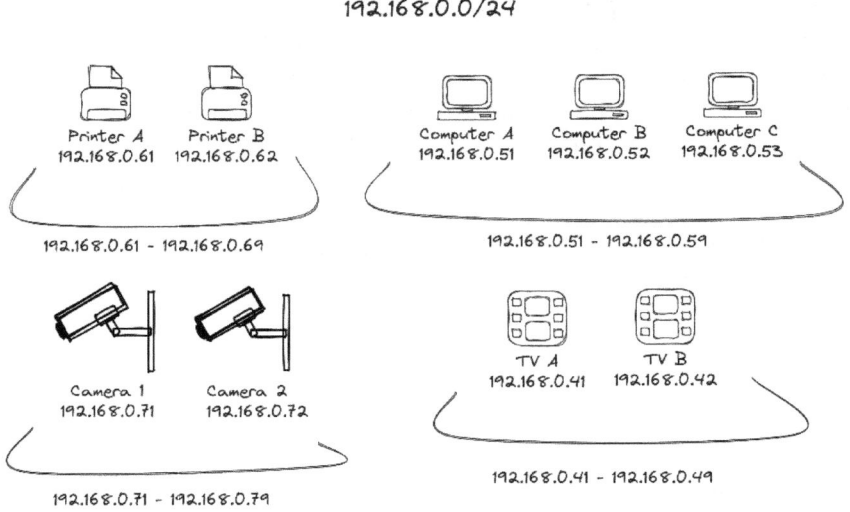

Remote Management

Remote management is an option that allows you to configure your router outside your local area network from far away.

Enabled ☐

HTTP: `8080`
HTTPS: `8181`

Remote Management Address (IPv4): 68.21.34.21

Allow remote access from: `70.70.70.65 / 65.65.45.58`

In simpler terms, this often refers to the internet, but it could also include other networks adjacent to an organization. This can pose significant risks if not carefully considered, especially for your home network where it is unnecessary. Therefore, you should disable it.

Here's a funny anecdote about this feature: Once, I received internet from an ISP that provided an edge router with this setting enabled. You can imagine my horror when I discovered it. Unfortunately, it took a few days to notice, as I was preoccupied with moving and all that.

DMZ

The acronym for this configuration is derived from the phrase "demilitarized zone."

Current DMZ Status: `Enabled`

DMZ Host IP Address: `192.168.0.100`

A DMZ in a router serves as a middle ground between a network's internal (i.e., local) and external environments (i.e., the Internet). You can define an IP that is static to a specific device, thereby "placing" that device in the DMZ zone. But what would be the use for this? Well, often in networks, we run web servers (i.e., computers) that host websites. We make them internet accessible so that others can view our website. However, the world is not a nice place, and many will attack those web servers. Think I'm exaggerating? Mine receives an attack every minute or so from all over the world. Others, like big organizations, have it worse. So, while we can be confident that these attacks won't be successful, we still think, "well, you never know." This is where DMZ comes in. Anything placed there is separated from the rest of the internal network, the place where we know we have valuable stuff.

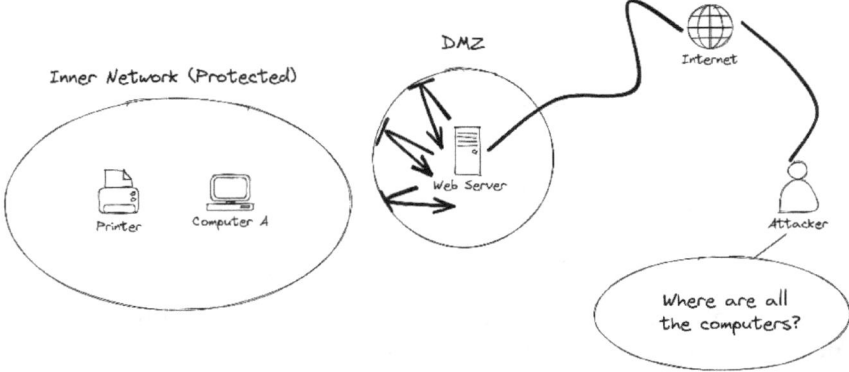

It is unlikely that you need a DMZ enabled if you are not running public servers. Then again, others use these to isolate other devices such as smart cameras.

Device Discovery

Device discovery is a featured enabled by a protocol called *Universal Plug and Play* (UPnP). It enables services to advertise their availability to other services in the network. The typical configuration menu looks like this:

UPnP:	Enabled
Advertisement Period:	30 minutes
Time to Live:	5 hops
Zero Config:	Disabled

When you enable UPnP on your router, the router broadcasts on your local network for any devices that may want to advertise such services. A few of these devices supporting UPnP will respond by providing information about their capabilities and services. This is how your phone can find your smart TV, gaming console, or network printer seamlessly for media streaming, gaming, or printing tasks, without requiring manual configuration of network settings.

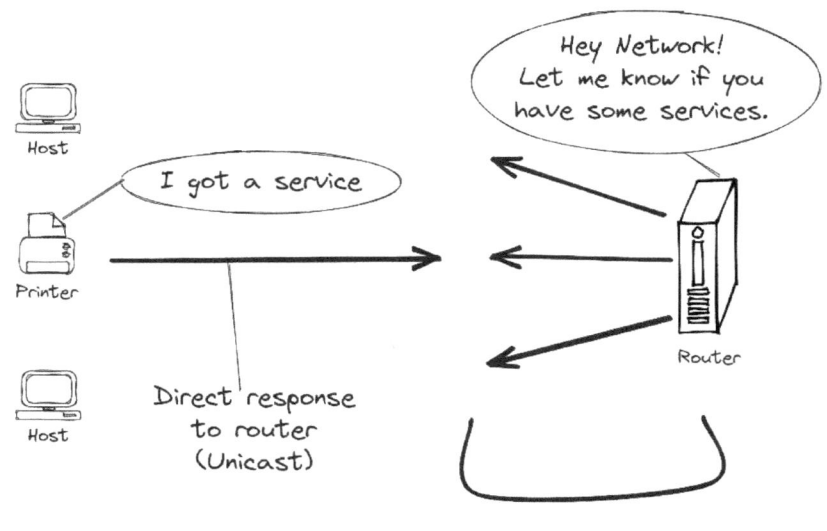

Broadcast

In terms of security, zero configuration (also known as zero config) for UPnP allows for the automatic configuration of services offered by different devices. Is the above protocol then a security concern? Well, sort of. The U.S. Department of Homeland Security released an advisory for all organizations to disable UPnP. Which makes sense from the perspective that even if disabled, you would lose some convenience and will have to configure some services manually, but it wouldn't otherwise affect you. The concern arises because of the way UPnP works, which allows potential attackers to discover what's on the network. Instead of an attacker having to find out what's available, all they have to do is listen for UPnP messages. This scenario presupposes that the attack is already in your network, which is not easy. Yet, the more serious issue is when some edge router manufacturers implement UPnP in such a way that services are exposed to the rest of the world. So, that printer that you wanted to be easily discoverable in your network (without having to remember its IP address) is now discoverable to the rest of the internet. Yikes! Think I'm exaggerating? I once ran an application that was accessed through a web interface. My router decided to let everyone online see this if they knew my public ISP-provided IP address. Then again, my current router does not do that and I have UPnP enabled. So, it's up to you. Enable or disable UPnP but make sure that you test that services within your network have not leaked to the rest of the internet. Likely there is a way to verify this and I have documented it in the companion repository. Finally, regardless, keep zero configuration disabled. Automation is good but it is good to maintain a bit of control especially in regards to what is happening at your edge router.

Examining other network devices

You will need to evaluate the rest of the network devices, such as your computers and laptops. We already covered these in Chapter 1, but we didn't cover a large category: Internet of Things.

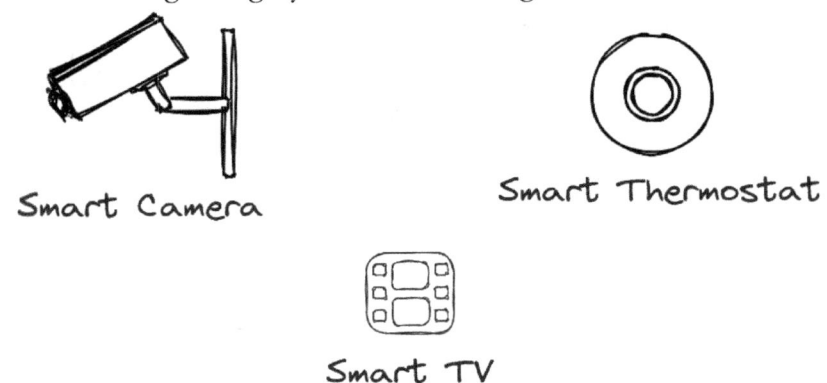

The Internet of Things (IoT) refers to the network of interconnected devices embedded with sensors, software, and other technologies, enabling them to collect and exchange data over the internet. These devices include your smart cameras, printers, game consoles, smart fridge, and others. As such, they are devices that generate a lot of network activity, and many have configurations related to their functions. For example, many have a UPnP setting, while others allow you to configure their IP address, although it's usually preferable to do that at the edge router. The absolute least you can do, even if you don't want to investigate all of their settings, is to identify them in your inventory list. Many organizations forget about devices that remain plugged into the network but are not in use. Think I'm exaggerating? Once, my students found old VoIP devices connected to a network, and when we reported it to the system administrator, he was equally puzzled since he thought they had been disposed of a while back.

Collecting data for network security

An essential aspect of detecting malicious activities within your network is to gather as many data points as possible. While conducting an inventory is beneficial, collecting data on network activity is even more crucial. In other words, understanding what's occurring at any given moment, such as who is communicating with whom, is crucial, but it's also essential to delve into the details at the device level. The companion repository offers specific examples of the equipment required to facilitate this process, but I also need to clarify some basics with you. Below is an example network, its devices, and the noise that each device generates.

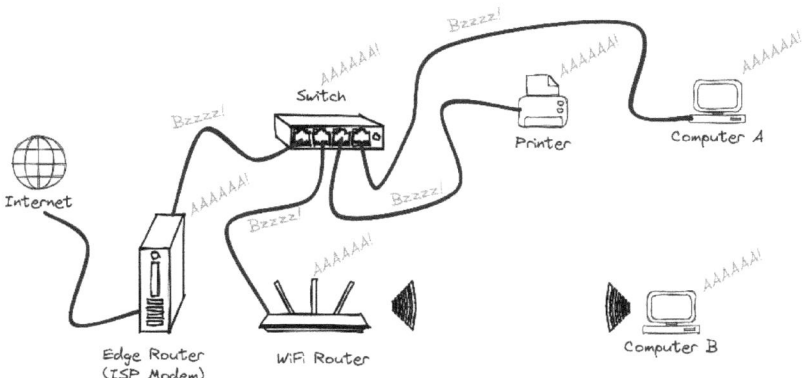

Capturing this noise involves collecting logs on a computer, such as antivirus logs or Windows events (e.g., login and logout). However, since this book focuses on networks, we will concentrate more on the data that is not typically collected from computers. Additionally, there are IoT devices for which network data collection is the only viable method, as they may not offer an easy way to collect logs. It's important to note that the description below applies to both computer (also referred to as host) data collection and network data collection.

In the image above, noise in the network is represented as noise on the cable. Capturing the data directly from your wired network will give you the best chance of observing what is happening. The industry term for observing network data is "tap" (as in "I'm tapping a phone line"). However, the question remains: which line should you tap?

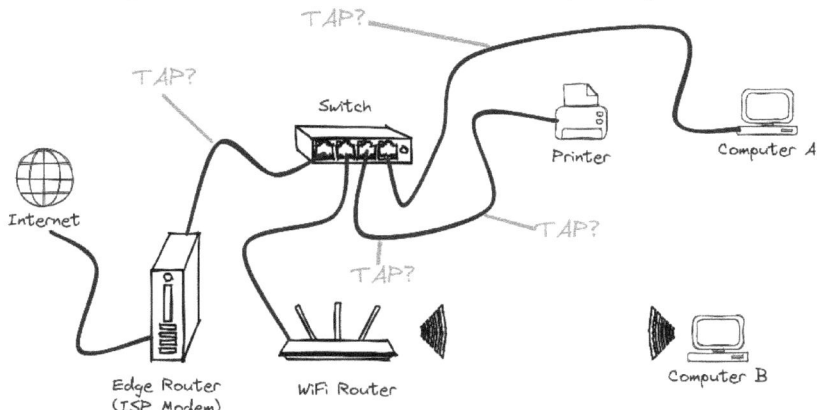

The correct answer is all of them. However, in the real world with budgets, the realistic answer is the one that gives you the most visibility of your network. I didn't randomly spend so many pages talking about your edge router. The closer you are to it, the more likely you are to observe communication between devices and the internet. What you will miss is device-to-device communication, but that depends on how the network is organized (i.e., its *network topology*).

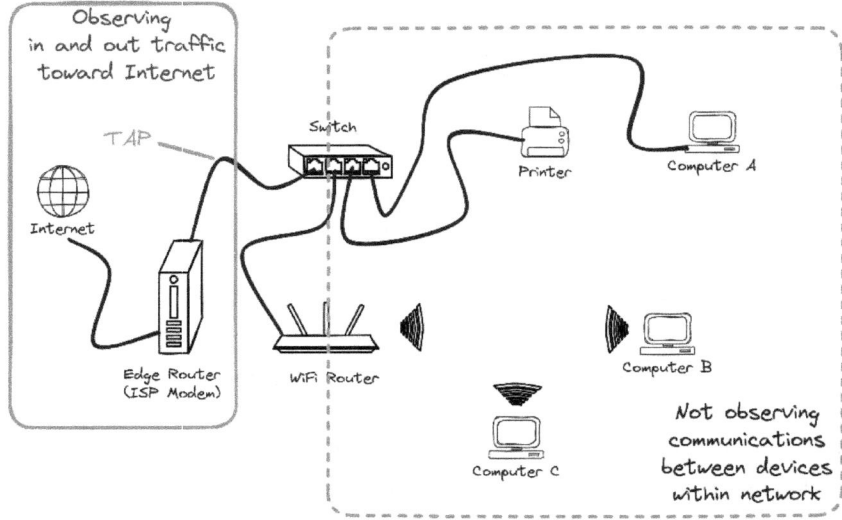

Alright, suppose you want to tap into your network exactly as depicted in the diagram above (i.e., adjacent to the edge router). How do you access the data?

To achieve this, we utilize a tap device or the port mirroring feature of your switches (also known as a *SPAN port*). As discussed a few pages earlier, port mirroring duplicates data from one port to another within a switch. Similarly, a tap device functions similarly, intercepting the data directly where the wire is "cut." In diagrammatic terms, here's a representation of a network tap:

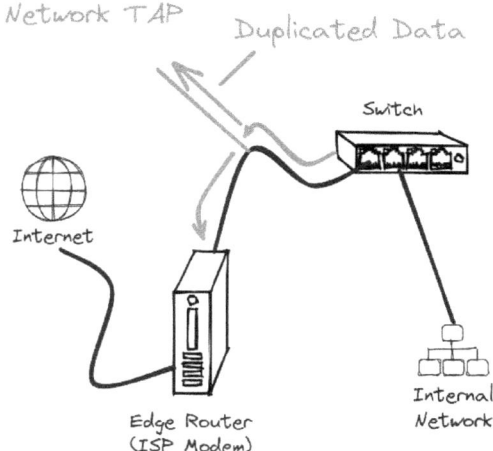

As a contrast, here's the same data duplication achieved using port mirroring.

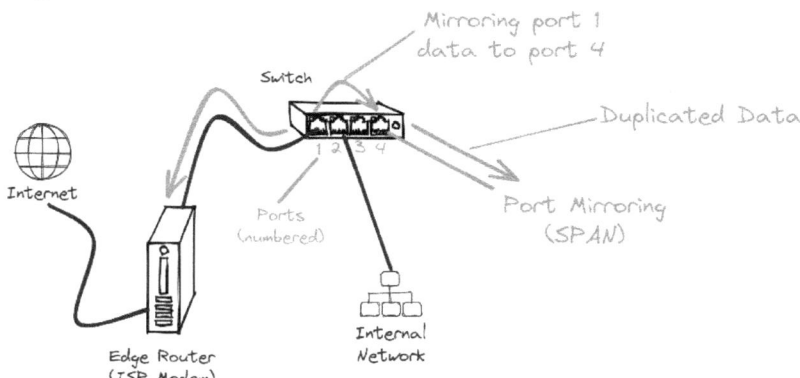

The next question is: what happens to that loose wire that contains all duplicated network data? We need a device to process all of this. Got an old laptop? It will do, although there are a few more options, such as single-board computers. There, you can install software that will process the network data and store it for you so that you can analyze it. It also performs some of the analysis ahead of time.

Most software that goes on this device is for Linux and is referred to as an *Intrusion Detection System* (IDS). We'll delve more into this in Chapter 7 but for now, all you need to know is that it can parse the network data off of the device's network card. The network card, in turn, is set into *promiscuous* mode. This means that the card will accept all packets, even those that are not meant for it, which makes sense since we have duplicated data that has a different destination than our IDS. Because the device runs an IDS, we often call this device an IDS, but other names have been used such as *sensor* or *collector*. I am going to use the term "collector" from now on.

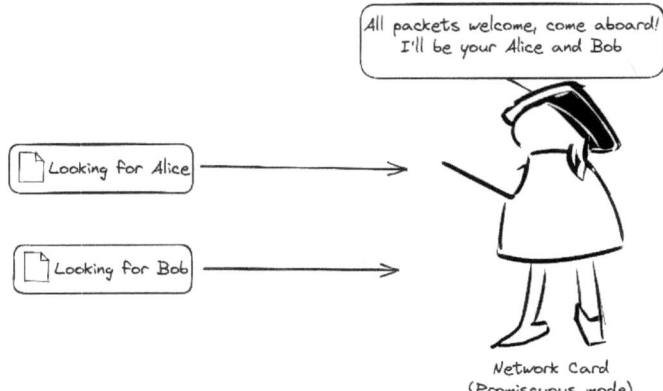

Where do we store all the data? After all, you may have noticed in your ISP's reports that on your network, you have a bandwidth (i.e., total bytes of traffic) of several hundred gigabytes. Well, we can store this logged data on the collector assuming there is enough storage. For your home network, this is more than adequate. However, for larger organizations, we store data on a separate computer or two, or better yet, on a cluster. A cluster simply means (I'm simplifying) many computers all operating as one.

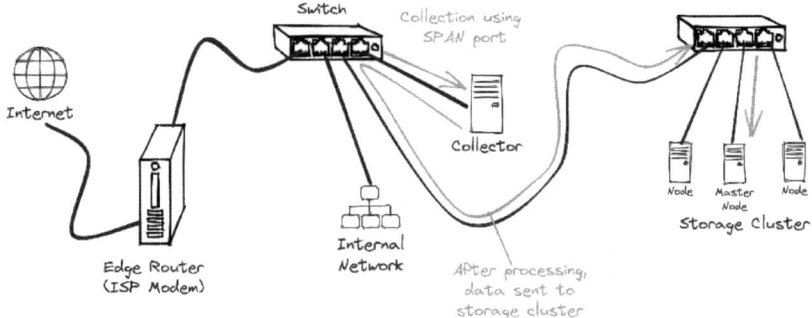

So, data is processed in a collector and then sent off for storage in a cluster. Then, you, the security analyst, come into the picture and need to access the data. You have two options: access it directly from the cluster or use an analytic stack installed on a separate machine.

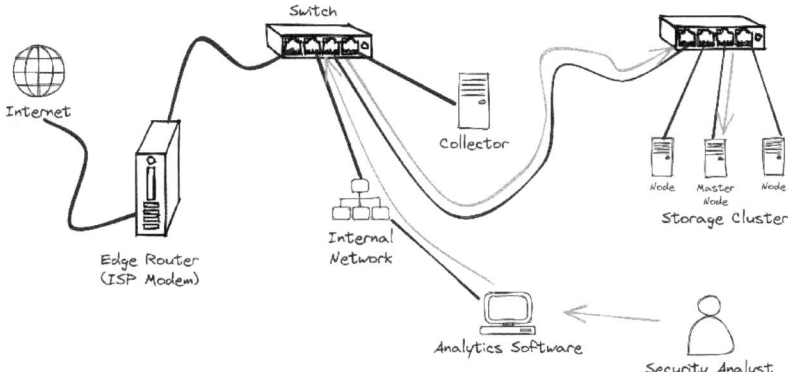

This way, you can now ask questions such as, "Which devices are using the most bytes in my network to communicate with another?" You can get an answer and determine whether this is reasonable. Setting up the above infrastructure falls under the purview of security engineers. I've had a few students who started off as security analysts and transitioned into supporting the infrastructure needed for security analysis. It requires a lot more experimentation than what can be covered in a book, but in the companion repository, I provide you with several options so that you can follow along, starting with setting up a collector/cluster/analytics stack on a single machine in your network, to practicing with virtual datasets on your computer.

Summary

- Modems, routers, and switches are the most basic technologies that constitute modern networks.
- Configuring modems is crucial for taking the first step in securing your network.
- Internet of Things devices are also devices whose network configuration should be considered.
- To establish network security monitoring, you need a tap device or port mirroring and a collector device.
- Security analysis is conducted by analyzing data via an analytics stack that accesses data stored in a cluster or similar storage system where data have been collected.

3 UNDERSTANDING THE BASICS OF TCP/IP

- Learn about how a packet goes from point A to point B over the Internet.
- Understand what encryption is.
- Explore basic network protocols that modern applications run on.

Overview

To learn to walk, you need to learn to crawl. This chapter is just that. You'll get through all the major concepts of how the internet works and what the most common protocols are. It is a bit of an information overload. Most people get overwhelmed with all the protocol acronyms and buzzwords. Focus on retaining whatever you can and do not stress if you can't remember everything. You'll see these again. As always, take the time to follow the exercises in the companion repository to gain practical skills in what is being discussed in this chapter.

Understanding the basics of network traffic

Time to get an understanding of applications and services and how they are observed in networks. You've already learned about IP and how packets travel through the internet. Now we will talk about applications. More specifically, say when you use a messaging app and you send a message to someone else across the internet, how does the computer know that the internet packet it received is for the messaging app as opposed to a video game or email app?

Network packets utilize ports to identify different applications. These are not the same as the physical Ethernet ports discussed in Chapter 2 but rather software ports. Each device gets a total of 65,535 ports that it can use for different applications. When we talk about applications and not internet packets, the data transmissions are classified as part of a connection (or flow). In other words, when you are making a video call, that is a connection to someone else's computer (or server, but we'll ignore that for now). For that connection to happen, a port needs to be used by the operating system. In fact, the other party to your video call also needs to have its operating system allocate a port.

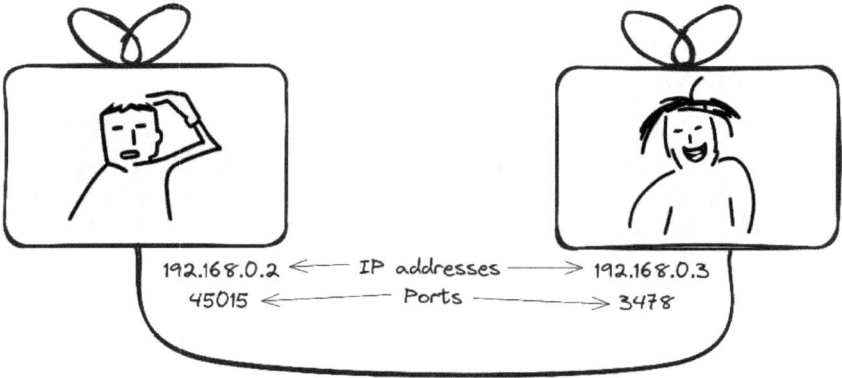

So, for packets to move from one point on the internet to another, you need not only a source and destination address but also a source and destination port. It gets even more interesting, though. We have two different protocols on how these connections should be operated by our computers: *Transmission Control Protocol* (TCP) and *User Datagram Protocol* (UDP). TCP focuses on replicating telephone communication in such a way that data is always in order.

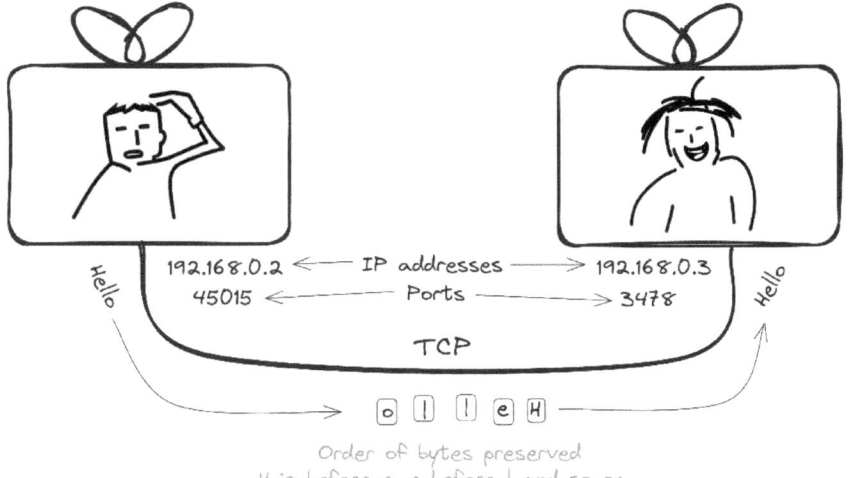

UDP, on the other hand, aims to provide real-time communication with no concern for order or lost parts of a communication. Operating a phone call over UDP could result in someone missing parts of a conversation and also hearing bits of the conversation out of order.

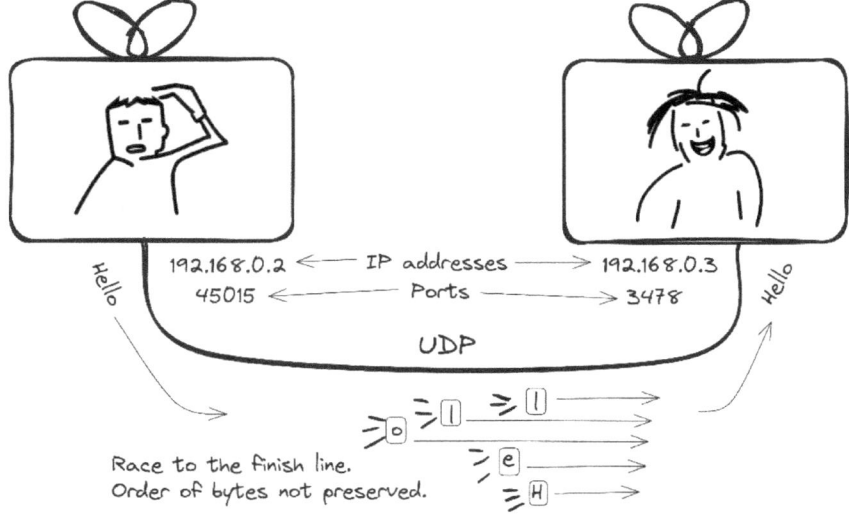

Sidenote, in reality messages contain several bytes so technically it is the order of messages (i.e., packets) that is not guaranteed, but for illustration purposes I feel single bytes make this race to the finish line more obvious.

Based on the above, TCP is considered the protocol that plays nice and has built-in congestion control mechanisms so that when traffic jams occur in a network, they can be resolved. TCP always waits to verify that the other party received the data. UDP cares little about other connections and can send an unlimited amount of data as it pleases. It is also the go-to protocol for attackers who want to overwhelm networks with network packets (i.e., *Denial of Service* attack).

Regardless, both protocols are used in networks today for different applications. In fact, when we refer to an application using a specific port, we also have to specify the protocol. For example, web servers use TCP at port 80 while network time synchronization uses UDP at port 123. Note that you can run two different connections on the same port number as long as you use a different protocol. For example, you can have both TCP and UDP on port 53. The two connections are seen as separate things.

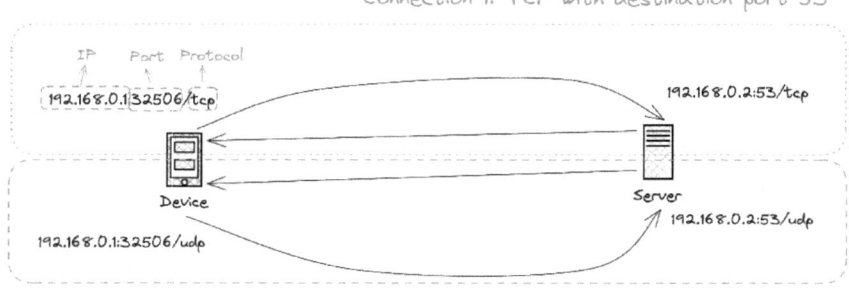

Connection 1: TCP with destination port 53

Connection 2: UDP with destination port 53

You probably noticed based on the above that a few ports are known and standardized. Ports starting from 1 to 1024 are considered standardized and used by specific applications historically. The actual range of standardized ports is larger, and organizations register these with the *Internet Assigned Numbers Authority* (IANA), which is related to ICANN, the entity that allocates IP subnets. Small world.

So, IANA has a registry for these ports. However, many people developing network applications don't bother registering the ports (or cannot). For this reason, there are several security websites aimed at tracking as many applications associated with different protocol/port combinations. Yes, malicious software uses ports to send data in and out of networks, and that is also documented. Here's an example of a report for a port:

Port 1243 Details — Bad stuff!

tcp — Trojans that use this port: BackDoor-G, SubSeven, Sub7(*), SubSeven Apocalypse, Tiles

tcp,udp — SerialGateway ← Good stuff!

In the passage above, you can see that port usage applies to both malicious and legitimate software. Therefore, if you encounter traffic under this port, you would need to conduct additional analysis to determine its nature. A detailed discussion will follow in a later chapter.

Now, let's delve into understanding how networking works. Imagine you want to connect to a website. If you use "http" in your browser (although you shouldn't), your browser will resolve the IP address of the web server hosting the website and will utilize port 80 (the standard port for http). The packet header leaving your computer will appear as follows:

Overall, we add headers with the information needed for the packet to be processed every step of the way, from router to router for layer 2 and 3 (MACs and IPs), and then for computer to computer for layer 4 (ports). Notice that I left empty the source port. It turns out the packet is not ready to leave your computer without a source port. Before this packets leaves the computer, a source port is also needed. What should your computer use? It could use 80, but that is standardized for websites. You are not hosting a website, but rather visiting one. The system could also pick one at random out of the 65,535 available. Well, almost. What happens is the operating system often has a range reserved for that purpose called the dynamic port range, usually comprising high-level ports. Windows used to allocate anything above 1025, but in later versions, it started allocating above 49,152. The choice of the number is not random since IANA has specified that ports above 49,152 until 65,535 are never allocated officially; however, unofficial or even malicious software can use any port it likes as long as it is not occupied by another active application. To make matters even more complicated, other operating systems may not adhere to this rule. For example, Linux distributions vary in terms of implementation, with some having their dynamic port range set between 30,000 and 65,535. So, in the above example, the complete connection information would look like this:

```
Layer 4       Src Port: 45123   Dst Port: 80
Header
TCP           Other TCP metadata goes here
```

The paradigm model represented by these connections is called client-server architecture. In this model, one side, the initiating side, is referred to as the client, while the receiving side is termed the server. For security purposes, it is important to differentiate between the two when examining a connection. With the simple rule presented here, you can easily identify both the client and the server, thereby knowing who initiated the connection.

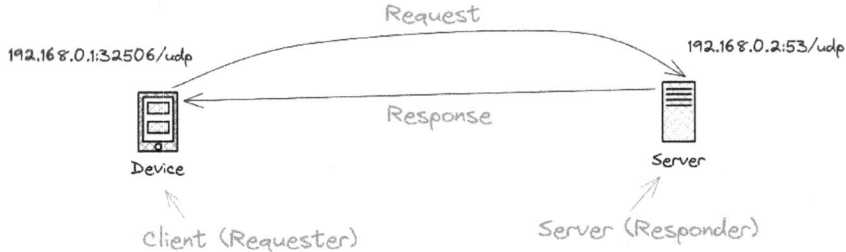

It is also useful to know which side is receiving because it indicates that it has a port 'open' to receive data. Then, we can start asking questions about whether that is expected. For example, if you see other computers connecting to your laptop on port 80 (indicating that your laptop is on the server side of the communication channel), you would have to ask why. Are you unknowingly hosting a website on your laptop? Or is it some malicious software?

Encrypted vs unencrypted traffic

As a security analyst, you will also need to identify not only the client and server (along with their associated ports) but also determine whether a communication channel is encrypted or unencrypted. Encrypted traffic is data that cannot be eavesdropped on by anyone other than those who possess the decryption key. Typically, this key is held by the two devices participating in the connection. For instance, a client and server can encrypt their communication to prevent unauthorized access to the transmitted information.

But you might ask, what's the big deal? If you enter your password on a banking website using your computer while at an airport, isn't it safe as long as your computer is virus-free and no one else sees your password? Well, when you enter that password and hit send, here's the path that packet takes:

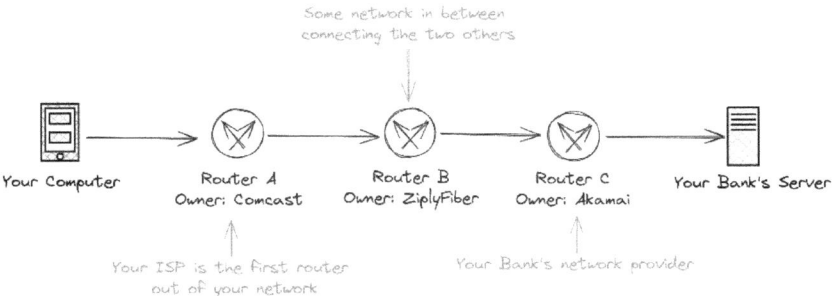

That involves several cables or wireless signals through the air and multiple hops through various routers—routers that you don't own, have never seen, and could be accessible to just about anyone. Yes, I'm entering paranoid territory, but come on, do you trust your ISP? Anyway, suffice it to say that it is extremely easy to monitor actions in an unencrypted channel. In fact, that's what Clifford Stoll did when he discovered a KGB hacker attacking military facilities in the early '90s. He connected a series of teleprinters that continuously printed what was passing unencrypted through the wires of Lawrence Livermore Laboratory. This laboratory was being used as a staging point for the attackers to pivot to military facilities.

```
$ login
$ copy all files
$ logout
```

Which brings us to an important conundrum: Unencrypted traffic is great for network security analysis but bad for overall network security. Every time a critical protocol implements encryption to ensure privacy, security professionals complain about how it weakens their ability to secure networks. However, more often than not, encryption and privacy prevail, resulting in a significant amount of network traffic today using encryption—some between clients and servers, and others being end-to-end.

Symmetric Encryption

Client and server encryption is straightforward: you connect to your bank and only you and your bank can see a password entered during that interaction. Encryption occurs using a commonly agreed encryption algorithm called a cipher. There are many ciphers, but the ones preferred for this type of communication are those that are both secure and fast, like AES. A cipher uses a key that needs to be agreed upon ahead of time between the two parties to the communication. Hence, this type of encryption is called symmetric encryption (both parties share the same key).

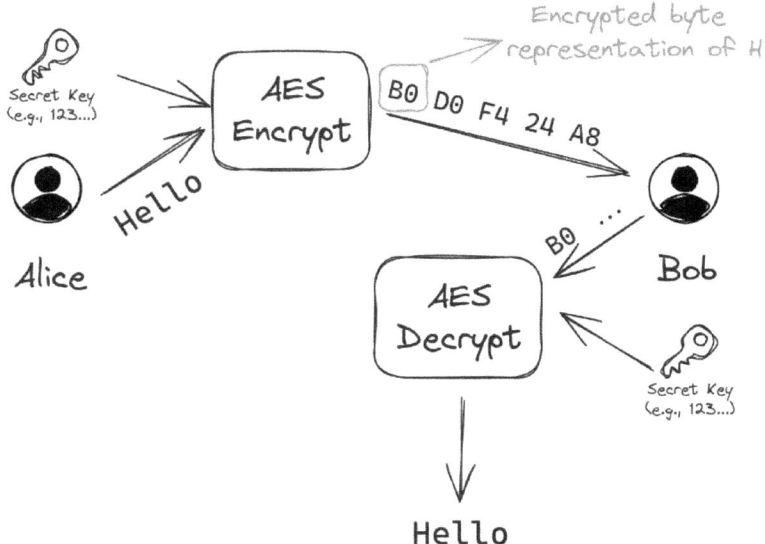

Public Key Cryptography

How is the key established? There is a second category of ciphers called public-key cryptography (also called asymmetric encryption). RSA is the most popular in this category. These ciphers are computationally expensive (i.e., slow) but have a unique property: they require two keys, one for encryption (public key) and the other for decryption (private key). Even more interesting is the fact that one party can distribute the encryption key, and as long as they hold onto the decryption key, they can decrypt anything encrypted with the encryption key. This means that a server can send their public key to the client; the client can use it to encrypt a randomly generated symmetric key, which they then send back to the server to decrypt using their private key. In this way, both parties now possess a symmetric key that only they know. This is what it looks like visually.

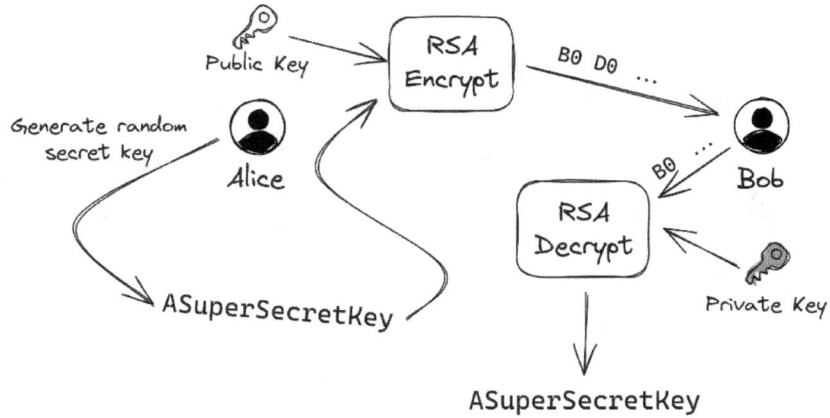

End-to-end encryption: Diffie Hellman

End-to-end encryption also makes use of a special kind of public-key cryptography to solve a similar problem. In modern computer networks, very rarely do two clients communicate directly with one another. Instead, servers are used as meeting points, and while the channels between each computer and server are encrypted (using the process described before), the server can, in theory, eavesdrop on the communication.

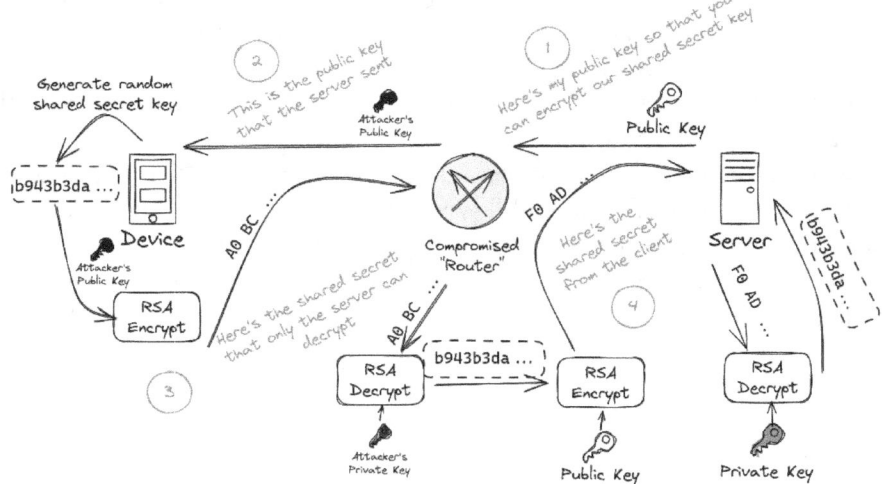

In the example above, notice that because of the router in-between swapping the public key for its own, they are able to identify the shared secret that will later be used for symmetric encryption (e.g., AES).

So instead, another layer of security is established using end-to-end encryption. This involves a special kind of public-key cryptography (e.g.,

Diffie-Hellman cipher), where two devices can generate temporary public and private keys separately. They then swap their public keys, use them to encrypt a portion of what will eventually become the symmetric key, and start communicating with each other. Even better, the server can detect this process happening, but without access to the private keys, it cannot determine the final symmetric key. If this sounds complicated, it's because it is—pretty close to voodoo magic, but it works. Here's how it looks in a diagram:

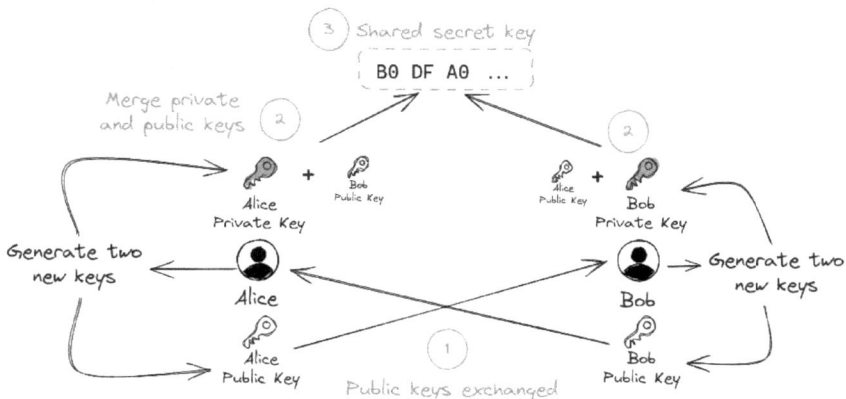

The math for this is even more complex, but as a security analyst, all you need to know is that when people talk about end-to-end encryption, that's what they mean.

One-way encryption: Hashes

Within the realm of encryption, there is a special category of hashes. You use hashes whenever you need to provide proof of integrity (i.e., something has not been modified) or when you want to protect critical data in the event of a data leak. The only downside is that hashing is a destructive process, so once something passes through a hashing algorithm, it often becomes a randomly looking alphanumeric sequence. On the bright side, the same input into a hashing algorithm will always return the same output.

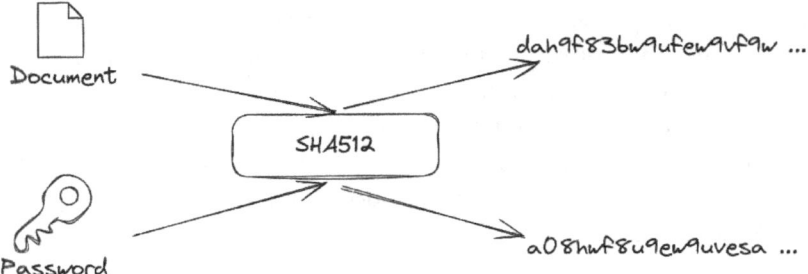

You will find hashes used in databases for passwords. In this case, a random fixed sequence is appended to the original password called the salt. That makes it far more difficult to crack the password should the hashed passwords ever get leaked. Typical hashing algorithms are bcrypt and PBKDF2.

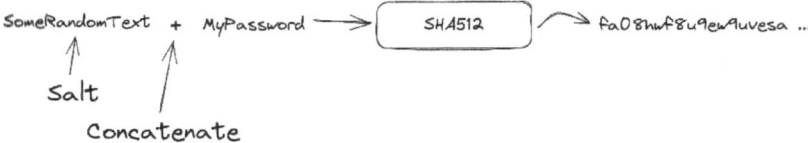

Integrity hashing uses algorithms that are typically fast and are meant to prevent someone from using a non-authentic or corrupted version of a file. For example, a file to be downloaded from a website will also provide its hash so that once downloaded locally, someone can quickly verify the authenticity of the file.

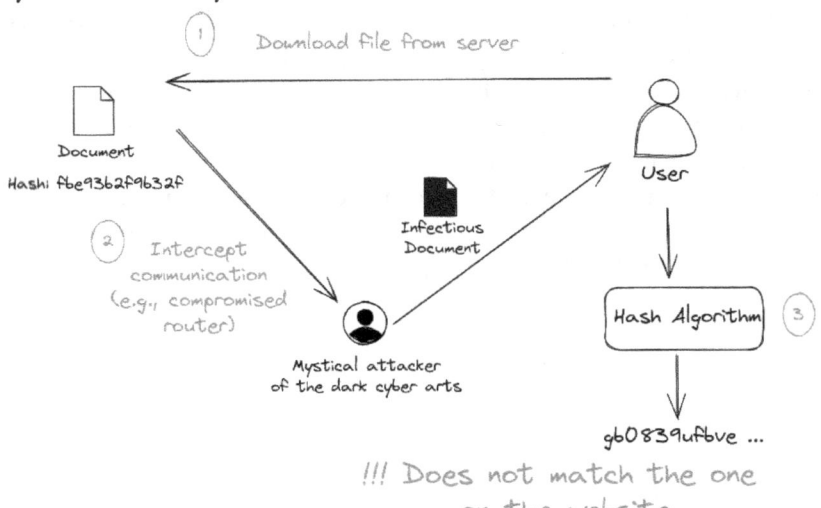

Signing and Identity

But there is a final big curveball when it comes to encryption. Before you start communicating via an encrypted communication channel with another party, how do you know that they are who they say they are? This is particularly important for end-to-end encryption since you may be talking to someone who you shouldn't trust, but even for classic client and server communication, it begs the question, how do you know the server is the one you are looking for?

Well, the solution to this problem is fairly straightforward. Remember public key cryptography? You can use it to sign things in such a way that the other party can verify their authenticity. The way this works is that if you have a document, you can hash it. This makes it smaller, typically a few characters long. Think compression but not quite since the process cannot be reverted. You can then digitally sign the hash, which is a representation of the original document. You do that by feeding it into the private key, and that will spit out an encrypted version of the hash. You can then start handing out your document (the plain readable text) everywhere accompanied by the encrypted hash (i.e., the signature).

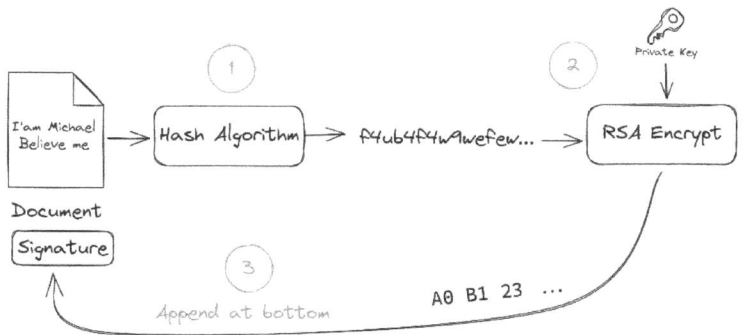

In case you are wondering, and I know you do, the hashing may seem like an extra step until you realize that it actually compresses a really large text (whatever that may be) to a much smaller hashed version (e.g., 64 characters long). This speeds up encryption too.

Anyone that receives the document can use your public key to decrypt the signature, which will give them the hashed version of the document. Then they can hash the document on their end and verify that the two hashes match. This works because any other public key would not properly decrypt the signature, and so it proves that the public key was a pair to the private key that was used to encrypt the signature.

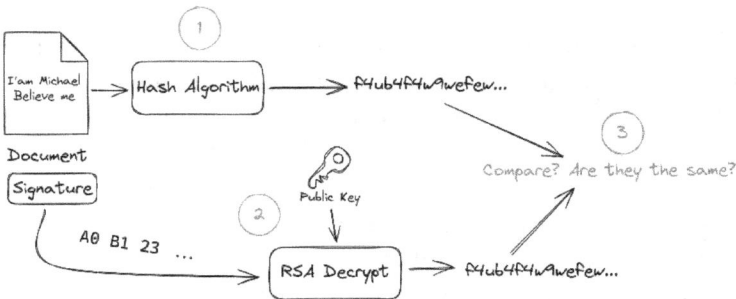

Still with me? Private key signs, public key verifies. Keep the private key private, distribute the public key. Turns out, you can use this process to sign everything: documents, domain names (e.g., google.com), or even your identity in a messaging app. Although, if you noticed, I have omitted to specify where we get the public key that is used for verification. After all, if I pretended to be Google, couldn't I craft my own keys and pass my public key as legitimate? Well, yes, so to solve this, we had to invent a trusted party, often referred to as a *Certificate Authority* (CA) in the context of websites. One well-known CA is Verisign.

The job of these trusted parties is to sign not documents but public keys of other people. The public key related to the private key of the trusted party that signs all the other people's public keys is then distributed and kept on all of our computers. Your operating system comes prepackaged with these public keys; that's how you can know that when you visit Google, you are visiting the right place.

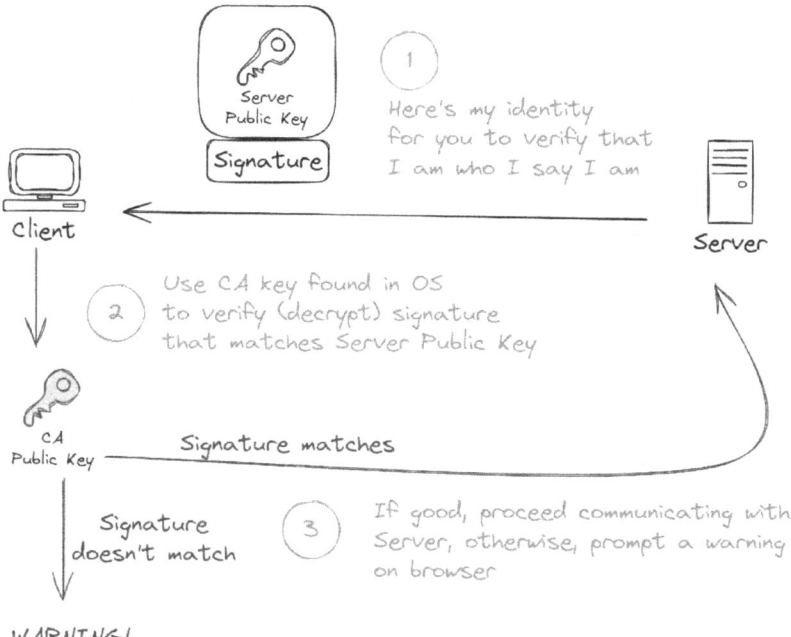

That is the whole point of using HTTPS on your browser instead of HTTP. It not only encrypts the communication channel between you and the server, but it also verifies ahead of time that the website you visit is who they say they are. The only large difference regarding the process described above is that newer versions of HTTPS use a version similar to Diffie-Hellman where new keys are generated for each session. This way, if by some unfortunate event the key is cracked, only one session of your network traffic to that website is compromised and not all. This concept is called forward secrecy.

Reviewing common services and protocols

Time to start connecting the dots on what you've learned in the previous two sections and how it will affect the work of performing security analysis. I'll be providing you with examples of common services and protocols that you are going to see in networks, and we will establish what ports they typically use and whether they are often encrypted or not. Also, if additional security measures such as identity verification through signing occur. We will talk about the following common network traffic services that you would observe:

- Domain requests (DNS)
- Web browsing (HTTP/HTTPS)

- File transfers (FTP/FTPS/NFS/SMB)
- Email (SMTP/POP3/IMAP)
- Remote login (SSH/RDP)

Note the associated protocol names in parentheses. There are many, and if this is the first time you are seeing this, it is a bit of an information overload. Don't fret. They will eventually become second nature, and that is also why I am using plain English to describe them.

Domain requests

Domain requests refer to question/answer type of traffic observed in networks where a computer seeks to find an IP address based on a domain name. For example, do you know what the IP address for Google's server is? Probably not. Could you memorize it? Probably, but why would you do that? Enter domain names (i.e., google.com). The *Domain Name System* (DNS) protocol consists of a client and server application so that you can ask for a domain name's IP address and get back an answer. A bunch of good Samaritans host DNS servers, and the DNS client that lives inside your OS is tasked with asking them frequently about different domain names.

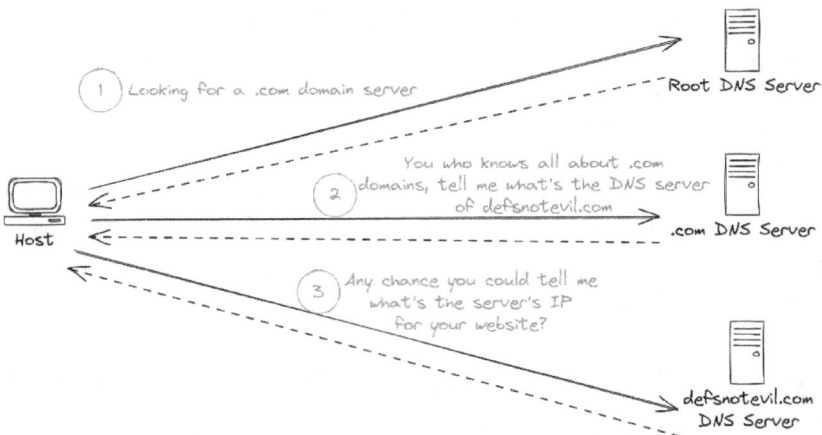

This may be some of the most frequently observed network traffic on nearly any network, typically occurring over port 53. Of course, there are networks hidden in dungeons that may not require domain names, but still. You will constantly see such requests from all network devices. Key points to know about DNS traffic in relation to security analysis:

- It is initiated by both humans and machines.
- Relay servers are often used in networks to speed up processes.
- Not all requests are visible in a network due to caching or

encryption.

The first point may sound peculiar, but it is crucial for security analysis. When observing network traffic, profiling what you observe is important. Similar to the TV show "Is It Cake?", your task is to determine whether a DNS request originates from a machine (i.e., program) or from a human. Using this perspective, you then need to determine whether this activity is benign or malicious (more on that later). Here's a visualization depicting DNS requests over time made by humans as well as by programs.

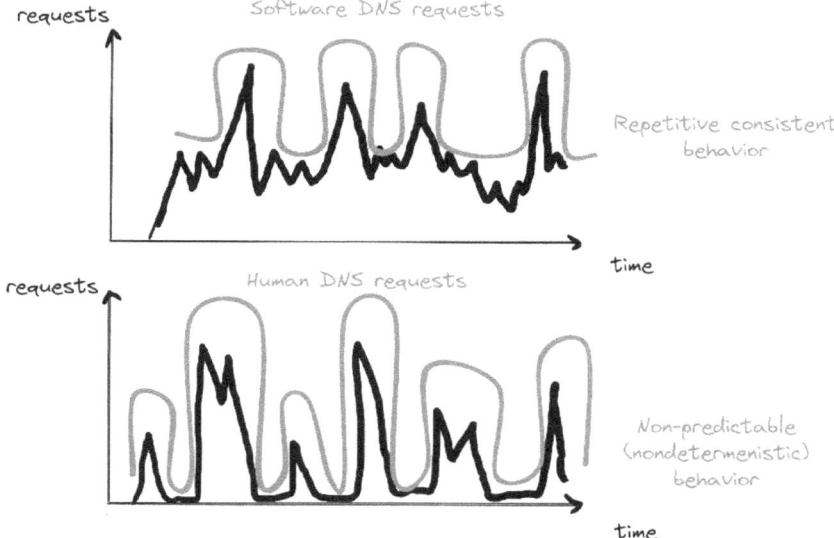

I've intentionally depicted things not as clearly defined because in reality that's how network traffic looks like, especially if you are looking across different devices. Having said that, notice that the human-initiated DNS requests have no periodicity; they occur randomly. The machine-initiated DNS requests are somewhat more consistent. The only factors that may break this pattern are whether a computer is on or off, or whether someone is active, such as during working hours.

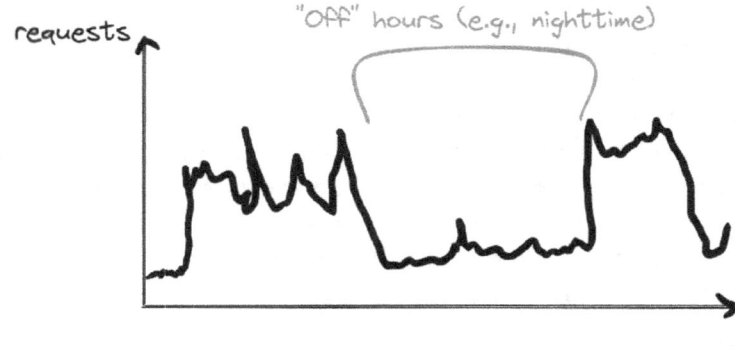

On to some more technical aspects. DNS requests are made in a hierarchical, reverse order. For example, if I wanted to find the IP address for the domain michael.tsikerdekis.com, a DNS server would typically inquire first about the location of .com DNS servers, then about tsikerdekis.com DNS servers, and finally about michael.tsikerdekis.com on that DNS server. The technical term for this process is called recursive resolution and it was shown earlier but here's a refresher.

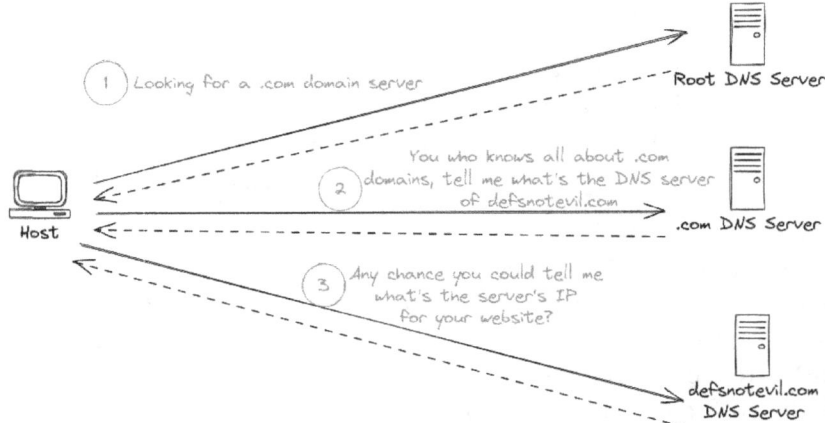

Because this process involves a lot of back and forth, a relay server (often either your router or your ISP) handles this exchange, so what you see on your network are DNS requests and DNS answers.

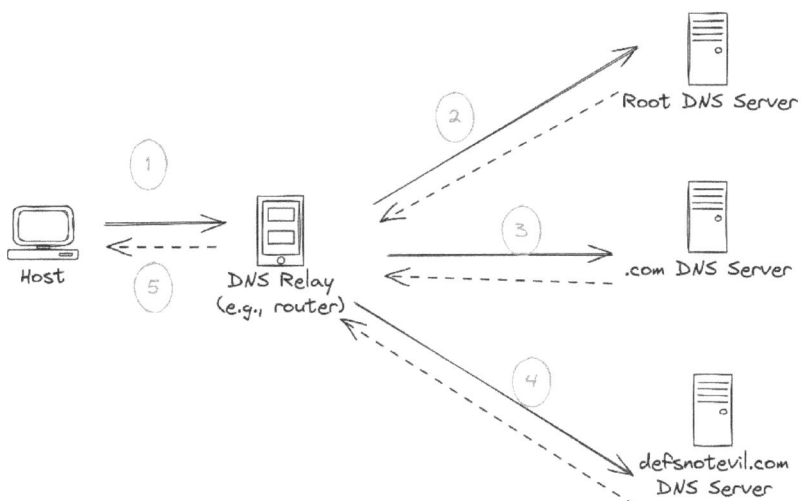

To make matters even more interesting, you may often type google.com into your browser, but no DNS request may occur because your DNS client caches (temporarily stores) previous DNS answers to speed up your internet experience. Even more complicated is the fact that while regular DNS is unencrypted, recent advances include encrypting DNS requests or sending them over other protocols (e.g., DNS over HTTPS). All of this becomes a factor in the analysis of the protocol. In other words, what you see in network traffic may not be all that happens within computers.

Web browsing

Web browsing became a thing with the advent of the HTTP protocol and the first browser back in the early 1990s. There are two types of web browsing: unencrypted over port 80 and encrypted (HTTPS) over port 443. The protocol is quite similar to DNS in the way that it is observed as traffic. A client (browser) contacts a web server to retrieve a website. Back-and-forth requests and responses occur between the two as someone browses the web.

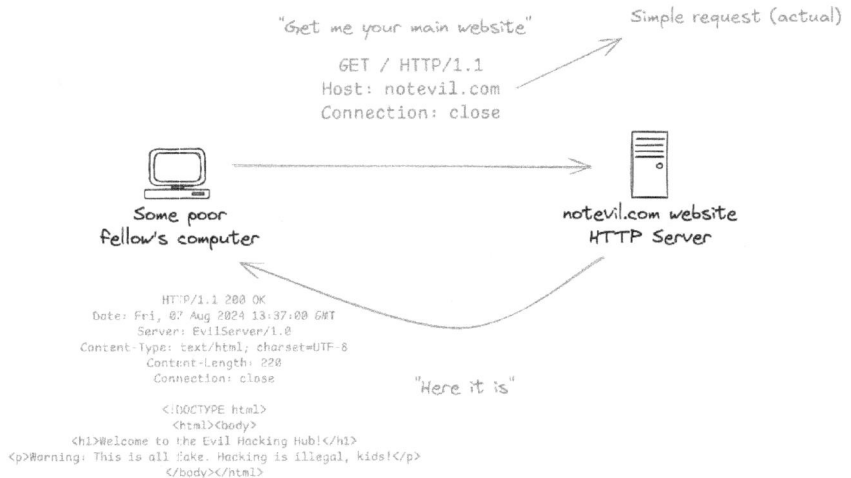

Much like DNS, its network traffic can be human and machine-initiated. Sounds weird? How does a machine browse the web? Well, software needs to complete several tasks with various servers. For example, your antivirus needs to download new virus signatures daily. The process of downloading happens through HTTP.

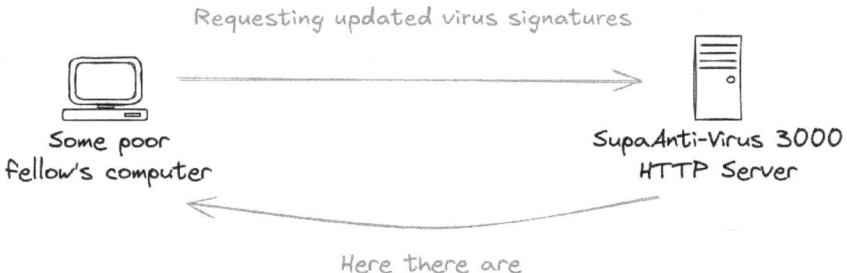

Even more interesting is the fact that browsers and other software may use caching to speed up the retrieval of pages. For example, things that remain static, like images, are retrieved only once. Subsequent retrievals are loaded from a cache. That effectively means that browsing to a website for the first time will generate more byte traffic than subsequent times.

File transfers

File transfers occur via several network protocols in a local network. These include the *File Transfer Protocol* (FTP) over ports 20 and 21. There is also an encrypted version (FTPS). This is a generic file transfer protocol, but operating system-specific file transfer protocols exist, such as *Network File System* (NFS) primarily for Linux, and *Server Message Block*

(SMB) primarily for Windows. These typically use ports 2049 and 445, respectively.

Whether you observe these protocols would depend on the network and the computers on that network. For example, in most home networks, you would not expect to see regular use of any of these unless file sharing occurs (e.g., someone shares a folder on Windows with the rest of the local area network).

From an analysis standpoint, you want to make sure that what is observed makes sense. Large file transfers would typically be classified as events of interest that should be further investigated. Often, such transfers are backups, but other such transfers could occur.

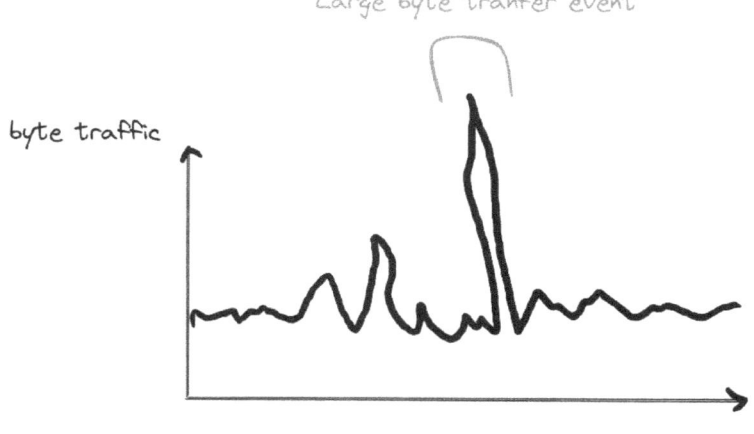

Typically these spikes distort the rest of the graph so they can stand out quite a bit depending on their size.

A final note for file transfers is that they can often happen over other protocols too, especially HTTP or even homebrewed protocols. What's the latter? A manufacturer makes an HDMI over Ethernet (i.e., video output but have it go through the network instead of a cable to the monitor), and they have to decide what protocol they will use and which ports. They decide to go with UDP (real-time protocol) and ports 2068 and 2066. Why these ports? Because reasons.

So if you see some random ports, how do you know that a file transfer is happening? Well, typically if you see a large volume, you would need to investigate either by checking physically the computer causing said traffic or by asking a system administrator in case you cannot do it yourself. Once, my students discovered transfers of 3TB daily in a remote network that we were monitoring through PISCES. We raised the issue with the system administrator, who confirmed that indeed this was

HDMI over Ethernet traffic. We made a note in our knowledge management software (a place where security analysts keep notes about what they saw for future reference) and ignored such incidents in the future since it was a known behavior of the network.

Email

Email traffic is almost exclusively triggered by human behavior, with software playing a lesser role. Yet, you may or may not see any on your network. "What?" you may say. Well, it depends on how you work with email.

Are you accessing your email through a browser and composing email through your browser? That's all HTTP traffic. You would see it going to a Google server if you are using Gmail, or a Yahoo server if you are using Yahoo Mail. Even more confusing, however, is that many email providers may just use Google's infrastructure to host their email websites and servers. Likely, you may see DNS requests ahead of the HTTP browsing traffic, and that would be a telltale sign of email activity.

On the other hand, if you are accessing your email via a phone app or email software on your computer, then you are extremely likely to see email traffic under the following protocols:

- Simple Mail Transfer Protocol (SMTP) on port 25; the encrypted version works on ports 465 or 587.
- Post Office Protocol version 3 (POP3) on port 110; the encrypted version on port 995.
- Internet Message Access Protocol (IMAP) on port 143; the encrypted version on port 993.

Overwhelmed? For now, just make a mental note that SMTP is for sending email and POP3 or IMAP is for accessing a mailbox. What about receiving? Well, the other side of SMTP is the "receiving" part of email delivery.

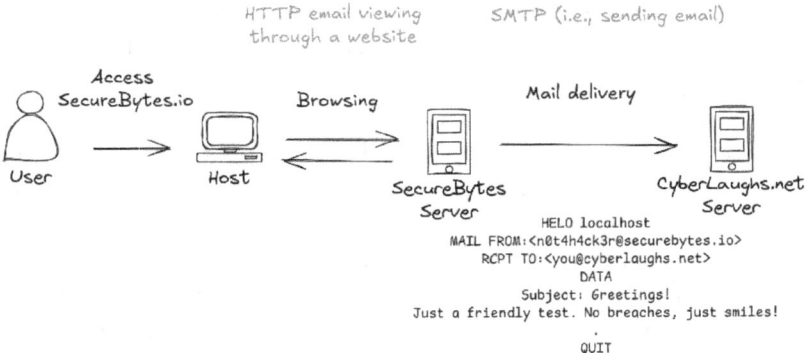

This has advantages and limitations in terms of what you can and cannot see. For example, if you are not hosting an SMTP server or the network you are observing does not have an SMTP server, then you are unlikely to see spam in network traffic (more on that in Chapter 5). You are likely to see, however, mail being downloaded periodically by your email software over POP3 and IMAP, as well as sending out email via SMTP. For example, if traffic is unencrypted, you will see that and can take action by checking the software's configuration. If large volumes of email are received (especially large attachments), you will also be able to determine that. Unauthorized attempts can also be observed over network traffic, even if the traffic is encrypted, by inference. In plain terms, if you see multiple attempts in a short time span of connecting on any of these protocols, then chances are you need to investigate further.

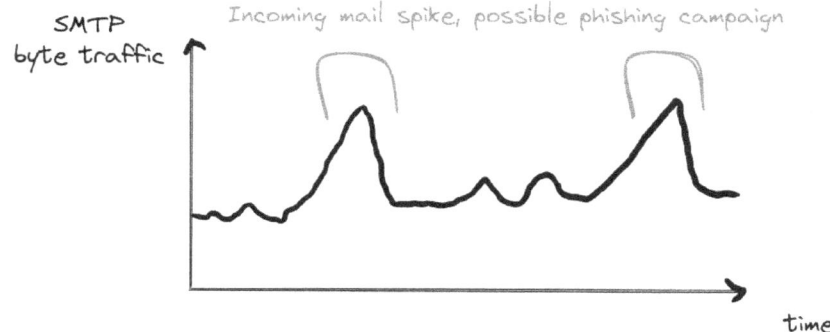

Remote login

Remote login protocols allow you to connect remotely to other devices, and in some networks, you are bound to see such traffic. This includes *Secure Shell* (SSH) for Linux over port 22 and *Remote Desktop Protocol* (RDP) for Windows over port 3389. Both protocols are always encrypted and human-initiated for the most part. These usually happen in sessions, and the volumes of data exchanged are small.

There is a slight exception to the human-initiated part. SSH has a file transfer version called SFTP. The port stays the same, but file transfers occur, so you can expect large volumes of data to be observed.

Here's a fun story. Given that these protocols are effectively backdoors to systems (assuming you can guess the username and password), many times system administrators change their ports. For example, for SSH, you can use 922 or 9922 instead of 22. Hackers would rarely be fooled by something like this, and in fact, it is easy to find out the protocol's port (more on that in Chapter 4). However, it does mitigate some of the excessive low-threat probing, which can often clog network traffic.

Your network's protocols

Profiling your network should be the first step in understanding what's going on. While this can be done holistically by observing NetFlow data (see Chapter 6), a good practice is to observe packet captures and determine the ports involved. Some software can even automatically recognize the software associated with various ports (e.g., Wireshark). For example, you can analyze a 24-hour period of traffic and list the total packets, bytes, and associated ports. This may look like this:

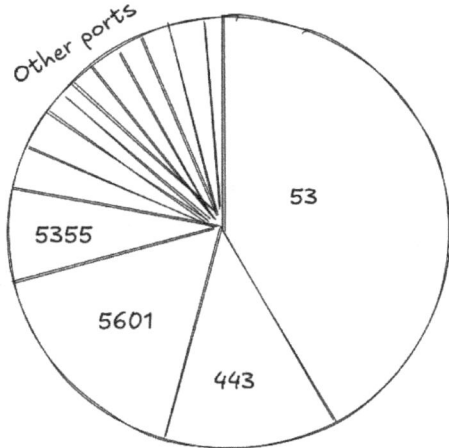

Example of top destination ports in network traffic

Then, the next task is to determine the types of traffic that you can recognize, such as email and browsing. In the image above, for example, 53 and 443 correspond to DNS and HTTPS traffic, respectively. After that, you can evaluate whether this is within reasonable bounds. For example, if you watched a movie on Netflix, several gigabytes of HTTPS traffic should be observed from a specific IP address related to your TV. Since you know why there is such high traffic, you can exclude it from the list and proceed to the next item.

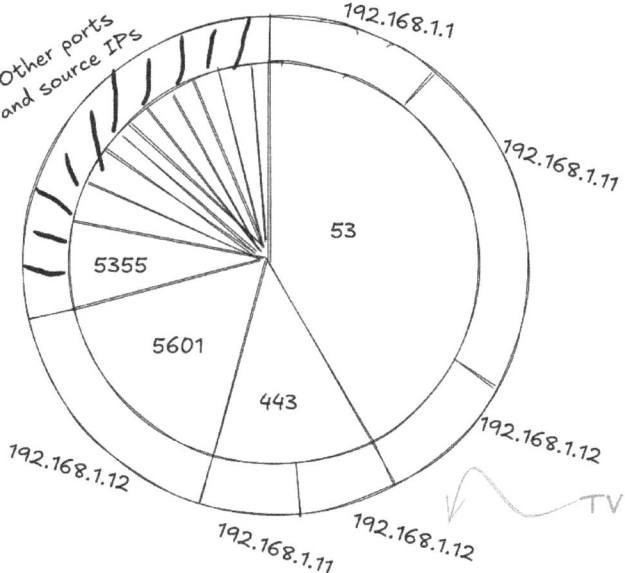

Example of top destination ports in network traffic

Once you eliminate all common services that have a reason to exist in your network, you will be left with a list of less common services. The next task is to start learning about these by searching online. Several websites can provide you with information about various ports and software commonly observed on them (including malware). Some of this is shown in the companion repository. The longer you repeat the process, the more you will eventually have a list of the most recognizable events in your network. These you will need to pay extra attention to.

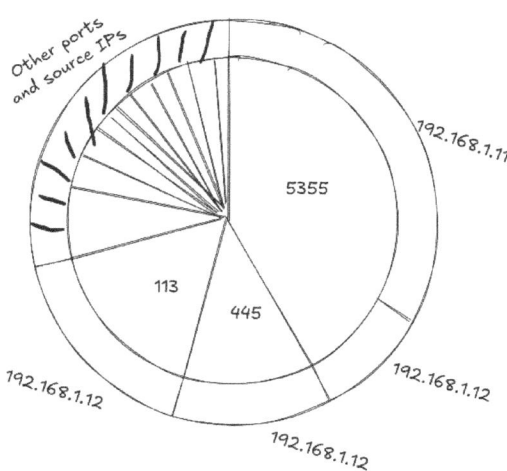

Example of top destination ports in network traffic

The above technique is called "Rinse and Repeat," and it is a useful way to manually evaluate a network. It is also useful because it can help you learn about your network. Repeating this once a day is a good exercise that will eventually not only teach you about your network but also about protocols that you may not have heard of before, which exist in your network. It will also force you to ask questions such as, "Is it normal that this software sends so many megabytes to its servers?" or "Why is this even running on my network?"

Summary

- Devices use 65,535 ports for different applications, identifying them in network packets through port numbers.
- TCP ensures ordered data transmission, akin to a telephone conversation, while UDP offers real-time communication without concern for order, making it ideal for applications like streaming as well as for Denial-of-Service attacks.
- Encrypted traffic ensures privacy, using symmetric encryption (e.g., AES) for client-server communication and public-key cryptography (e.g., RSA) for secure key exchange.
- DNS resolves domain names, HTTP/HTTPS is used for web browsing, FTP/FTPS/NFS/SMB are used for file transfers, SMTP/POP3/IMAP are used for email, and SSH/RDP are used for remote login.
- Profile network traffic by observing packet captures, identifying recognizable services, and evaluating their reasonableness to detect unusual or malicious activity. Rinse and repeat for ongoing network understanding and security monitoring.

4 SECURING YOUR ENDPOINT DEVICES

- Learn what the endpoint devices in your network are and how to best secure them.
- Learn about the principles of penetration testing.
- Gain a perspective on how to identify the behaviors of these devices.

Overview

The topic of the current chapter is about any devices connected to your network—sort of. We are focusing on devices where people interact with them and are connected to the internet. You likely have a few of these devices, but I wanted to provide a perspective that some networks may have many more than what can be found in your own network. However, since your network is closer to your heart, it will serve as a good point of review. So, while reading this chapter, you may want to focus more on the elements of your own network and ponder these. As always, a few examples are provided in the companion repository with more active exercises.

Understanding Endpoint Devices

Endpoint devices, in the simplest of terms, are all devices that sit at the end of communication channels (not the edge of your network). These include computers and laptops, but also increasingly other internet-connected (smart) devices such as TVs, fridges, temperature sensors, and security cameras. Your cell phone is a separate category of an endpoint device as well.

What's interesting about these devices is that they are assets in both the tangible sense (they cost money to replace) and the intangible sense (they hold data that might be difficult to replace or are critical). So, naturally, you would want to put in effort to protect or monitor these.

Let's start with protection. For computers, laptops, and similar devices, there is basic security hygiene, such as installing antivirus software and ensuring that a firewall is running. I'm calling these tasks basic not because they are easy per se but because they are common. The companion repository includes some examples of how you can set things up.

Protecting other types of devices is a bit more challenging. These devices often run proprietary operating systems or open-source operating systems like Linux, but with restricted access. Additionally, they often have low computational capacity and other energy-saving needs (e.g., if they operate on battery power). All this means that they are not easy to secure using traditional methods. However, you can and should evaluate their settings. I will mention two settings to check on most devices: remote access and updates.

Many devices have some mechanism to allow remote access, which is often enabled through a mobile app.

So, even if it is not a direct setting, you need to evaluate the degree to which remote access can easily be achieved by a potential attacker. For example, if access to these devices requires an email for the mobile app, consider whether your email is public. Do not assume it is not; chances are it may be. If you use a username, make sure it is not easily guessable. For example, my bank used to allow the following options for usernames:

- First name
- Last name
- First and last name
- Common words
- Email

You may say, "Well, they don't have my password, so all is good." However, imagine if someone started trying a bunch of random passwords against that username. The bank would eventually have to block the account, and when you need to access it, you won't be able to. It would be locked. In other words, you granted the attacker the ability to use the system's defenses against its legitimate users. This can be referred to as weaponizing or co-opting the system's defenses, and it is a common strategy for availability attacks. In this case, it is a *denial-of-service* (DoS) attack on your bank account. So, use a username that is not easily guessable along with a strong password.

You will also need to check and enable automated updates on these devices. You might think that this is something enabled by default, but it is not. I've lost count of how many devices would manually ask me to confirm a security update. Yes, this can be disruptive if it cannot be scheduled at a convenient time, but it is often necessary.

The final endpoint device you need to keep an eye on is your phone. Why is that different from your laptop or desktop? Well, three reasons: you move around with it a lot (even within your network), you are more likely to leave it exposed, and it is the primary device you use for two-factor authentication.

So, here are a few things to keep in mind for your cell phone, aside from keeping it updated:

- Use a password to lock its screen (no fingerprints, face recognition, or any biometric methods). A PIN works well; make it as long as you can remember, or a password would be even better.

- Encrypt its contents (to be fair, you should be doing that for most of your computers). There are different levels of security for encrypted phone storage (or computer storage). The best option requires you to input a PIN (or password) before the device can boot up and decrypt the storage.

The above two steps are more important than what people usually do with phones, which is to attempt to track them when they get stolen. In other words, they measure the tangible cost of the phone and underestimate the intangible cost. The reality is that a stolen phone's value lies in the fact that it can contain enough information for an attacker to access many aspects of your life, including your work documents, bank accounts, and other private, potentially irreplaceable information.

Completing an inventory of your devices

You may or may not have completed an inventory of your endpoint devices in the past. Or perhaps you think you know all of them; however, if you put some thought into it, you will see that you may have missed a few. Regardless, now is the time to answer the question: How many devices do I have that are communicating with the rest of the network or the internet?

There are several ways to determine this. The naive way is to go around and start looking. A better way is to check your router's connected devices list. This should account for most devices, but depending on the device, it may not be accurate. Over the years, I have seen many routers that undercount, especially if devices connect through a secondary router.

Connected Devices

MAC Address of Network Card →
b4:ad:a3:57:cb:e0 (192.168.1.212)
fa:f5:f2:1f:92:02 (192.168.1.98)
96:57:ca:1a:bb:ae (192.168.1.69)
8a:22:e4:ba:fc:bd (192.168.1.25)
58:d9:c3:56:04:64 (192.168.1.155)
 ← Assigned IP (Local)

There is another way. We can just ask these devices or, otherwise put, scan for them. But what exactly is network scanning? Well, we cannot go around and shed digital light. So, when we talk about network scanning, what we often mean is a program that checks different devices for their presence. Because devices have a network name and an IP address, the program queries different IP addresses to see if something is there.

Scan Results

✓ 192.168.1.212
✓ 192.168.1.98
✓ 192.168.1.69
✓ 192.168.1.25
✓ 192.168.1.155

Scanned 192.168.1.1-254 (253 addresses)
6 hosts up

The most common tool that has been used for years is Nmap, but there are others. In actuality, nmap uses several approaches to determine the existence of a device. It can use Internet Control Message Protocol (ICMP), a diagnostic protocol used by many devices to determine conditions in the network. However, other protocols can be used, such as Echo, which exists as both a TCP and a UDP version under port 7. Most operating systems have a service running on that port so that they can reply to Echo messages. This is also called pinging, or as a verb, "pinging a device."

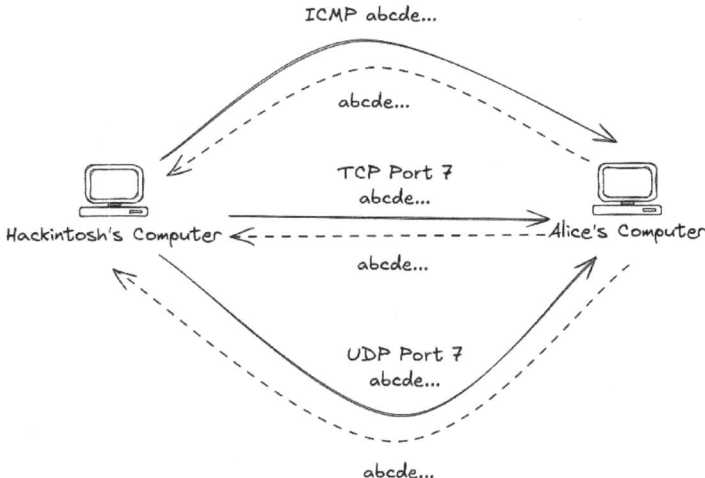

So, when you use nmap to scan a network, the program pings different IP addresses and waits for a reply. What happens next is a bit complicated, so a diagram is more appropriate.

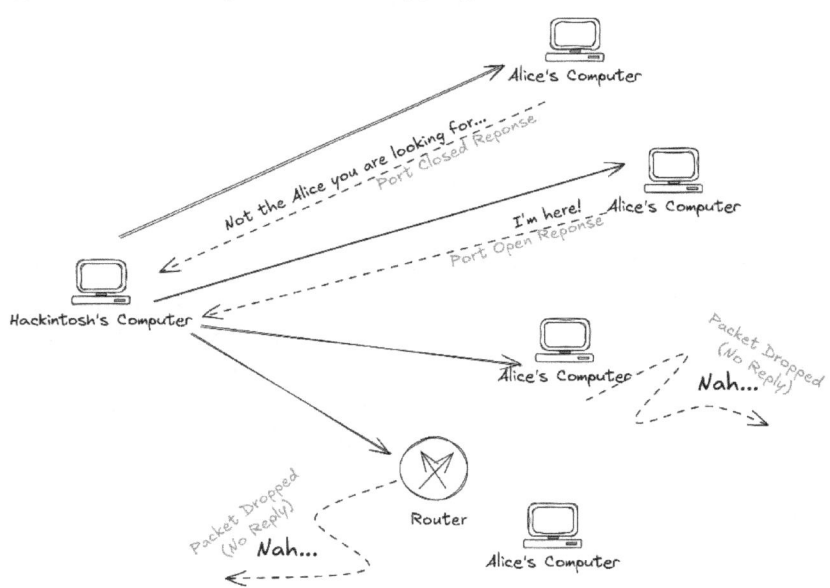

You can see four different scenarios. A negative reply, a positive reply and then two cases where there is no reply. That's right; something may be there but may not feel like replying. Frankly, though, nmap is quite reliable at finding things. In fact, aside from pinging on port 7, it can actually attempt to send arbitrary packets to any port from 1 to 65535. It can do that for each IP in your network. Why is that useful? Well, if a computer is programmed not to respond to pings or a router is configured to block pings, the computer may still be available and running. A database may still be welcoming new connections on a computer that otherwise does not respond to pings. Or even worse, malware may be lurking and awaiting connections on some port of your laptop. Either way, knowledge is power and all that.

After you complete a full network scan using `nmap`, you may find results like the following:

```
Scan report for 192.168.1.1

PORT       STATE SERVICE
53/tcp     open  domain
80/tcp     open  http
49152/tcp  open  unknown

Not shown: 997 closed ports

Scanned in 268.24 seconds
```

Conducting penetration tests

Your next task, once you know which devices exist in your network and are waiting for connections, is to run more specific tests to determine how vulnerable they may be. After all, by now, you've probably noticed the number of open ports everywhere. It is natural to wonder whether all these doors provide a way for an attacker to get in. This is where penetration testing tools come in. To be fair, this is not typically part of a security analyst's job, but it is important to understand this process since you will see it happening in networks that are monitored.

So, what is penetration testing? It involves taking a list of known vulnerabilities and running them against computers that have open ports susceptible to these vulnerabilities. For example, here's how usually a report looks like for a piece of software:

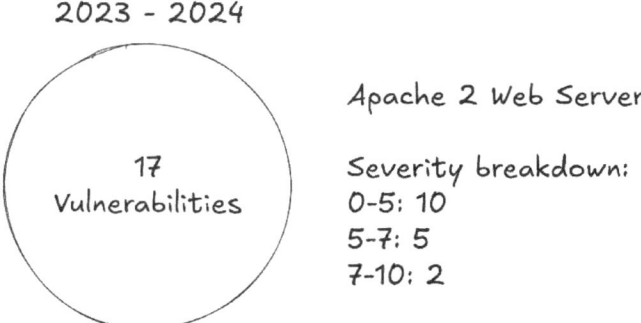

The severity usually reflects the impact if the vulnerability were to be exploited. These typically are not exhaustive either. They are more like highlights of vulnerabilities. For example, *Apache2*, a popular web server, has a total of 2,283 vulnerabilities throughout its lifetime. Sending packets to test each one of them just for a web server is a bit of overkill, especially when some of them are years old and likely patched. Also, not all vulnerabilities are equally severe. For example, consider these two:

- Current Vulnerabilities and Exploits (CVE)-1999-0926: Apache allows remote attackers to conduct a denial of service via a large number of MIME headers.

- CVE-2021-40438: A crafted request uri-path can cause mod_proxy to forward the request to an origin server choosen by the remote user. This issue affects Apache HTTP Server 2.4.48 and earlier.

Depending on your experience with web servers, you may or may not understand the specific terminology, but you can probably guess which one is more severe. It's the one from 1999. Most CVEs are assigned severity scores, and that one received the highest, a 10! Not to be outdone, the other CVE scored a 9.0. Of course, not all CVEs are as critical as these, so there's no need to test for all of them—just the ones that an attacker is likely to exploit successfully.

When it comes to software, not all penetration testing tools are created equal. Some can perform more advanced scanning than nmap, while others can go through several steps in the testing process. The more advanced tools can even reach the stage of privilege escalation (i.e., becoming an admin on a compromised machine).

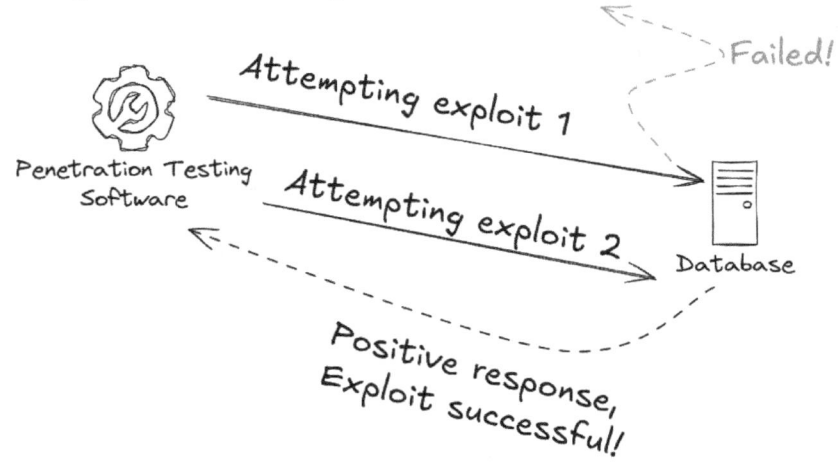

What you need to know is that regardless of the tool, these will only tell you if there are any known (emphasis on known) vulnerabilities on your network. They will produce a report, and if it says that you are all clear, it basically means that you are likely okay, for now. But that's fine since you keep an eye on your network for that reason.

In the companion repository, I demonstrate using some of these tools on your network. A final and important note: Networks that you monitor often have established penetration testing routines. These vary from frequent (once a week) to less frequent (once a year). The latter is the bare minimum required to pass an audit, but it's not the best strategy for obvious reasons. Regardless of the frequency, penetration testing creates noise. As a security analyst, you should see red lights go off, alarms firing, and alerts flooding your dashboards. This way, you know that your defenses are working because you noticed something suspicious (like a machine running a bunch of exploits). Attackers are rarely that noisy, but it's good to consider penetration testing a readiness exercise.

Penetration testing doesn't only occur when you initiate it (or run a script). It also frequently happens through scanning activity by attackers on a network.

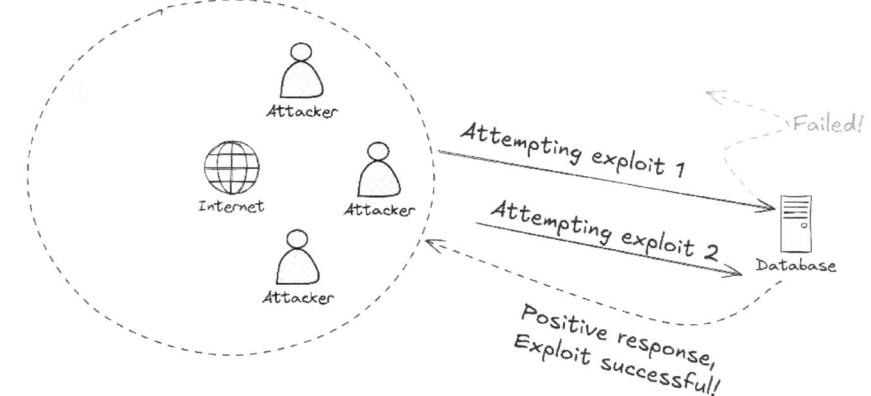

Real-world example: When devices talk to others using UPnP

Devices communicating with each other is nothing new. In fact, devices on your network are expected to coordinate for various services, especially when using UPnP. As a refresher, this is the protocol that allows devices to discover the services they offer. For example, a web server might say, "Hey, I'm here," or your Smart TV might announce, "Hey, I'm here if you want to screencast your phone to my screen."

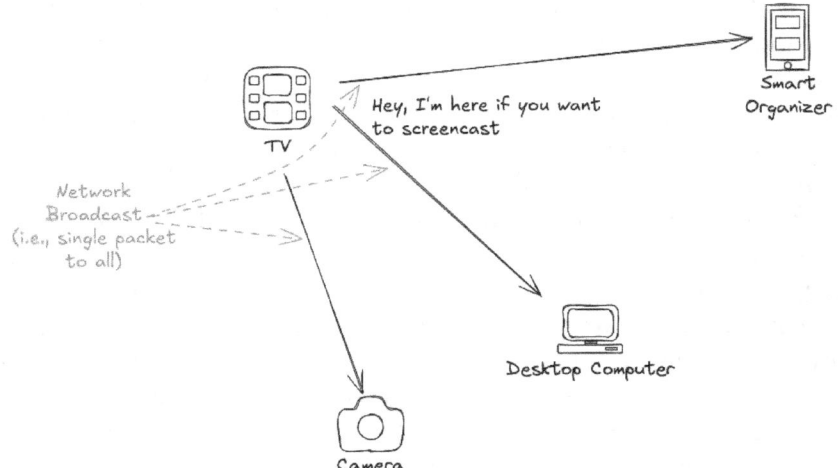

If all these communications happen within an internal network, then typically, there is no cause for concern, or so one would think. However, in 2020, a vulnerability was found in UPnP that allowed for a specific kind of attack: a reflection attack, also sometimes called an amplification attack. This type of attack exploits an existing infrastructure's vulnerability to target a specific victim.

To understand the attack, you need to understand the objective, which is denial of service. An attacker aims to disable a machine providing some service (e.g., a database). The attacker could use their own computer to target that machine and send 1 Terabyte (TB) of data.

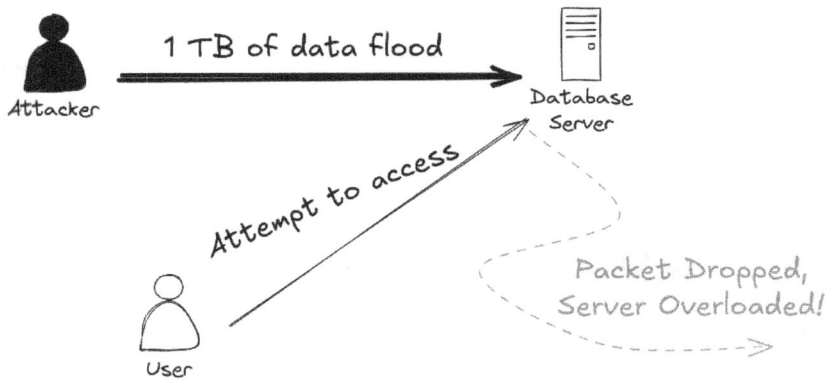

As you can guess, the receiving machine only needs to reject packet after packet. Easy. Then, the attacker gets ten machines and does the same.

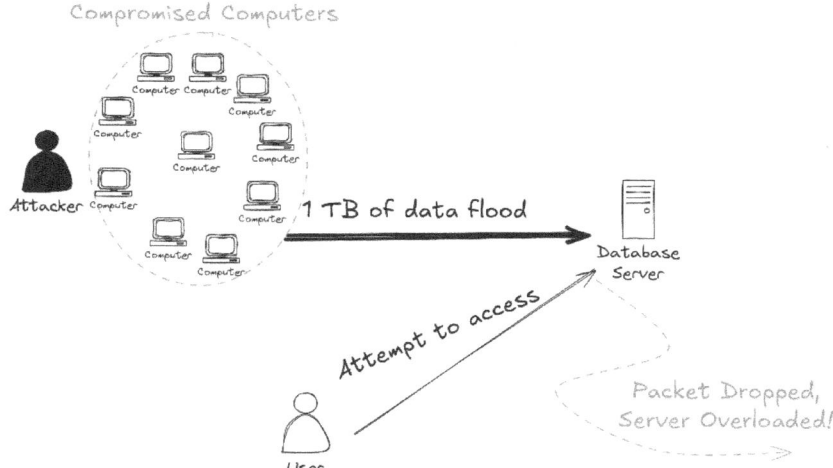

Now it is more difficult for the machine, but not impossible. However, the FBI catches on to this, and assuming the attacker is in the US, they descend and disable his or her equipment. If the attacker is abroad, then cross-border interactions and local laws at the attacker's location have to be taken into account. Let's just say, the attacker can often get away with it. But ten machines are just too expensive to operate, so what if the attacker could use someone else's machine?

Enter the UPnP vulnerability. CallStranger allows for exploiting UPnP subscribe messages that the protocol uses to send events to devices that have requested them. An attacker sends a subscribe message, and the UPnP service replies back to the victim's computer. The whole thing works because, on the internet, the source and destination IP information on the packets is not verified. So, if a packet claims that it came from some IP, the receiver will respond back to that IP.

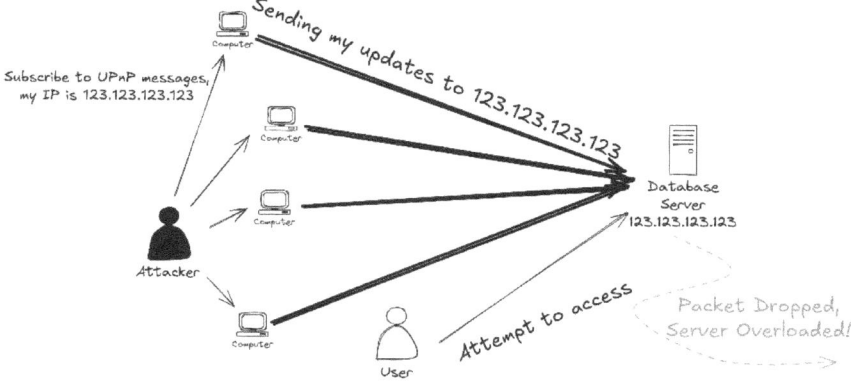

You may think, what's the big fuss? Well, the trick here is that the attacker sending the subscribe message is sending 100 bytes (this number is used for illustration purposes) while the response may be 1,000 bytes or more. This is a 1,000% increase in data. Pretty good deal if you are an attacker. If you can find a few more UPnP servers like that in a network, then with the amplification of the data response, you can overwhelm a target. Hence the name, amplification attack.

Likely, this vulnerability has been patched, but UPnP is probably still in your network. In the companion repository, I have an example of tracking it down and observing its hopefully benign activities.

Final note, amplification attacks are very common and typically involve tracking vulnerable servers. They are used for Distributed Denial of Service (DDoS) attacks. Servers that communicate over UDP are the most vulnerable to this attack since TCP requires a handshake, making an amplification attack not easily achievable.

So, a good practice is to keep an eye on devices that may expose services to the internet (more on that in Chapter 5), but it is also important to monitor your internal network. You never know when you might encounter a malicious visitor who could ask you for your Wi-Fi password.

Real-world example: Got a time? NTP and similar protocols

Watching what devices do on the network can tell you a lot about them, and sometimes you can actually discover that they shouldn't be there. I'm going to set the stage for this one. During an undisclosed quarter, my students monitored an undisclosed customer. Ticket after ticket and alert after alert turned out to be false positives. All normal. Most networks experience no incidents most of the time.

To give them something to do, I told them to investigate various protocols on the network. This is similar to IP fingerprinting (i.e., determining open ports on a computer and guessing what it is used for). But in this case, I wanted them to compare protocol traffic per IP.

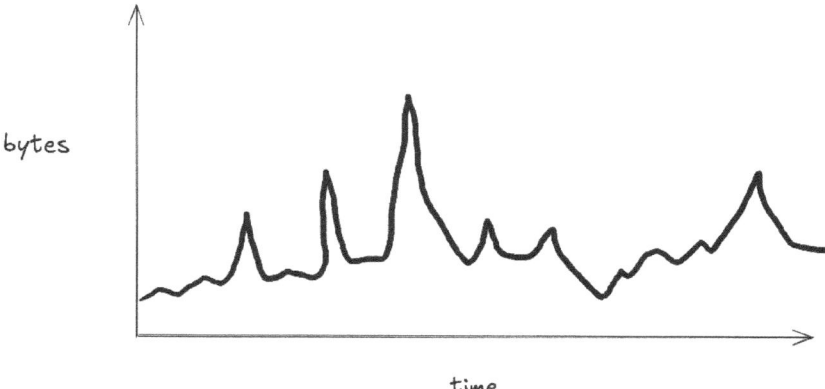

So, just like in the image above, a student showed up and said that the *Network Time Protocol* (NTP) traffic was a bit higher on that device than on other devices. For context, this is the protocol that automatically synchronizes your computer (and other devices') clocks. It consists of a request for time and then a reply.

It was a bit odd, but at the time, I had not heard of any active attacks using the NTP protocol. I looked it up, though (Google "NTP CVE"), and found several vulnerabilities, but not enough to be paranoid about. Yet odd is odd, so I figured we should explore further. For the record, security analysts often do not have local access to the network they are observing. This was the case for my students, so if they needed to investigate further, we would need to escalate to the local system administrator working at the undisclosed customer's site. Before escalating to the city, we did our due diligence. We needed to determine the 4 Ws:

- Who are the offending devices (IPs)?
- What is the protocol involved and what is the device? NTP

and unknown (could fingerprint effectively).
- Why is this happening? Speculative suspicious behavior.
- When is it happening? More specifically:
    o How often?
    o Does it follow a human or machine pattern?
    o How long has this been happening for?

The last question with sub-questions was what we needed to answer. My students pulled data on the past month's activity on the network and plotted graphs of the NTP traffic across different devices. We also measured and compared volumes of data (i.e., bytes) and requests (i.e., whether the offending devices were making more frequent requests). At some point, paranoia got to me, so I used my own network (which I monitored) to benchmark the same answers.

It turns out that my Wi-Fi extender (the device that extends Wi-Fi coverage) was making NTP requests much more frequently than any other device on my network. At least we knew that this behavior was not unusual and was likely benign. For whatever reason, however, I couldn't let it go, so I forwarded (escalated) the case along with all the data my students collected to the customer's system administrator.

They could have easily dismissed my case, but out of curiosity, they decided to investigate further. A day later, I got a response in the mail. It turns out the IPs belonged to Voice-over-IP (VoIP) devices (Cisco SPA112) that the customer used to provide phone service over the internet. They were benign; however, they were not supposed to be on the network. The customer stopped using them a long time ago, but the devices were not only left connected, but they also fell behind desks. Suffice it to say, the system administrator took care of that right then and there.

You may be asking, if the devices are benign, then what's so bad about having them connected to the network? Well, if you made a bunch of keys to your office, gave them to people you trust, and then forgot about them, wouldn't that be a concern? The keys still exist and may fall into the wrong hands at some point. Devices connected to your network are always on and may carry vulnerabilities. This is true for your computers too, but the major difference is that you maintain your computer (hopefully). Devices that you have forgotten about and that remain on your network are definitely not maintained (at least by you). They could become an attack vector (i.e., Trojan horse) for your network. That's why an inventory of your network devices is so important.

Summary

- Endpoint devices are the most critical points to monitor in a network. After all, they are likely to contain critical assets such as valuable data.
- Scanning for open ports can help you verify if there are any network points of entry to these devices.
- Penetration tests can help you establish whether there are active vulnerabilities in these devices that an attacker may exploit.
- Creating an inventory of endpoint devices, open ports, and vulnerabilities is an important task for securing a network.

5 EVALUATING THE PERIMETER

- Learn what edge devices are and which settings you should be paying attention to for them.
- Evaluate traffic patterns at the edge of the network to identify concerning indicators.
- Discover points of entry to your network through the network perimeter.

Overview

Security perimeters are everywhere in the real world. They are used in military settings to protect infrastructure, in convention events to regulate points of entry, at airports, and so on. Networks are no different. Aside from your endpoint devices, which can be compromised, there may be "cracks" in your perimeter that an adversary could exploit. Finding these cracks can be a challenge since, at the end of the day, traffic occurs between endpoint devices and rarely at edge devices (e.g., routers). However, there are likely some ways to determine what's happening through their settings, open ports, and other traffic patterns.

Checking network edge devices

Network edge devices are internet-facing devices, and you need to ensure they are as secure as possible. By now, you are probably aware of your edge modem/router and some of the configurations; however, there are some key critical aspects we need to discuss from a security perspective. These include *Network Address Translation* (NAT), port forwarding, and firewalls.

Let's start with NAT, as it is a key piece of technology that not only expanded our capacity to connect more devices to the internet but also provided a minor layer of security as a side effect. NAT is used by default in most cases where you receive internet from a larger ISP in your home, and many organizations use this technology to differentiate the internal network from the outside world.

To understand this better, let's consider a counterexample. Suppose you are a large organization and have requested an IPv4 subnet for your network. You are given the 140.160.0.0/16 range, which provides about 65,000 IP addresses for devices within your organization. But what if you are a university? If you count all devices, including transient student cell phones, you are likely to max out your available address space. From a security standpoint, it is also risky to use public IP addresses in such a way that anyone on the internet can probe any of your devices.

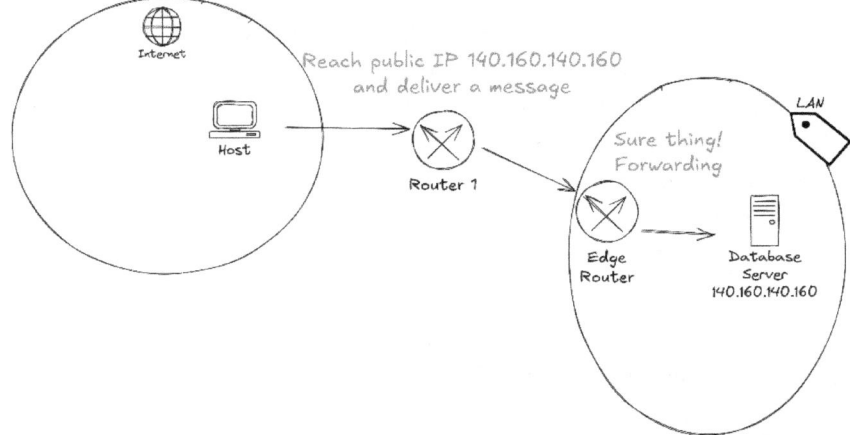

Enter NAT. The idea is that your network can have a public face or multiple public faces using one of the IP addresses within the 140.160.0.0/16 subnet block, and then internally, you will use private IP addresses. "Private?" you may ask. Well yes, RFC1918 is a specification from the IETF (the big folks managing important Internet things) that says the following subnets are private:

- 192.168.0.0/16
- 10.0.0.0/8
- 172.16.0.0/12

Even better, you can use these and chop them into smaller subnet blocks and create a hierarchy in your network.

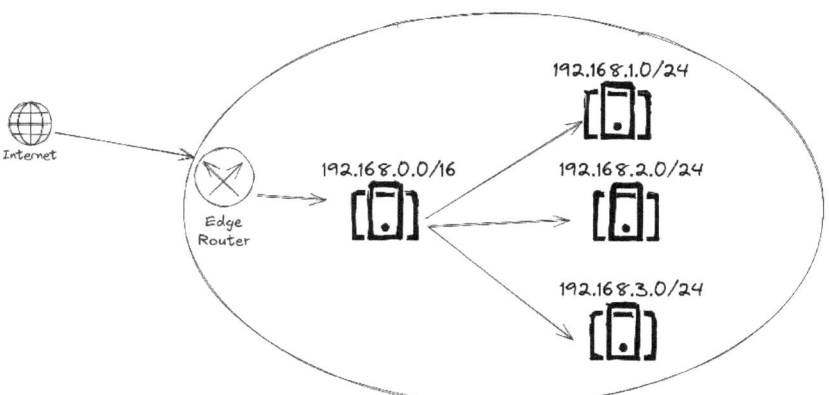

There is a big caveat for these IP addresses: routers won't forward them. That is, if the destination is within the private subnet block, they will deliver the packet, but they will never send it outward toward the internet. That's a good thing since your 192.168.0.1 may be someone else's too. So, how is your computer able to communicate with, say, Google.com? Well, NAT (Network Address Translation) translates packets coming into the network and going out.

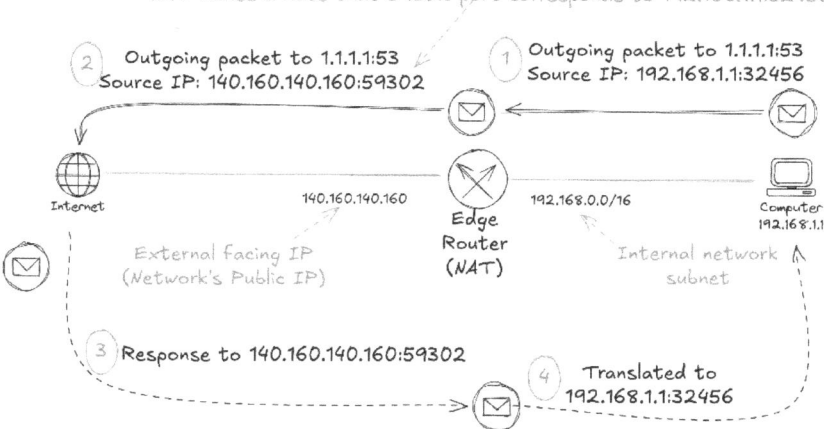

Notice in the diagram above that an outgoing packet with a specific port is replaced with another port (rewritten) once it's out on the internet. This way, if two people are communicating using the same port on their computers, NAT will be able to forward packets to each one of them since the port on the public-facing part of the network will be different. Fun fact: this public and private facing aspect also exists in human cultures. The Japanese refer to the public face you show to the world as "tatemae" (建前), while the private face is called "hon'ne" (本音). Pretty cool, you may say, but what does this have to do with security? Think of someone sending an unsolicited packet to your network.

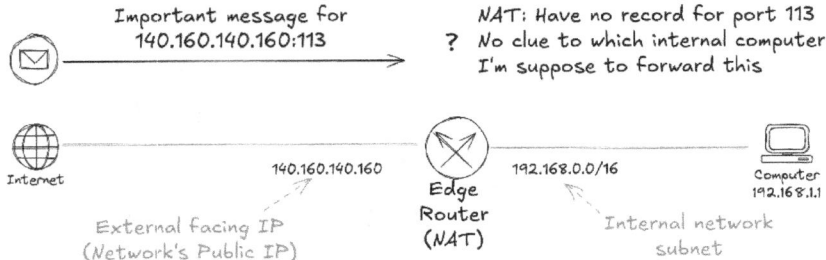

What is the router running NAT supposed to do with such a packet? Nothing. The packet was sent to your network, but which internal computer is the final destination is a mystery since NAT has no such record. So, logically, the packet is disregarded. It hits a figurative wall.

This is one of the biggest changes to modern networks that did not exist a few decades ago. Computers often have private, non-routable IPs and sit behind NAT, making it impossible for an external computer from the internet to reach them. Consequently, this means a backdoor opened by malware on a computer is not reachable from the internet and thus useless.

That leads to a change in behavior for ambitious malware developers. Where opening a backdoor to connect to a computer was the popular trend of the 90s, today's malware opts to bypass this NAT restriction by using *Command and Control* (C2) communications.

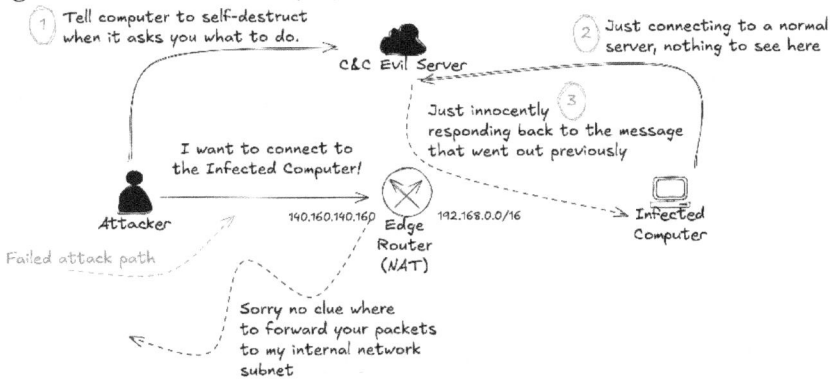

The big difference to note here is that the malware is reaching out to a server to receive commands, rather than the attacker connecting to the malware from the outside to give it commands. The end outcome is the same, however—that is, malware is bad either way.

There is also a big exception to the "backdoors don't work on private networks from the internet" rule. If the internal network has publicly reachable IPs for its host machines, then these machines are reachable from the internet. Here's an example:

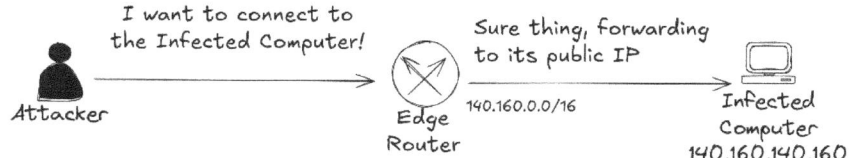

Notice that there are no private IPs involved and that public subnets are used even for the internal network. In such cases, which ideally should not exist and are generally considered poor practice, a firewall serves as the next line of defense, and it often resides in a router.

A firewall is a software or, less often, a hardware device that is configured with rules to determine which packets are allowed in and which packets are blocked. The same applies to packets leaving the network. There is specialized software for this, but for the purposes of security analysis, we will focus primarily on basic firewall functions, as they may impact the security of a network and how it is monitored in terms of network traffic by a security analyst. By the way, the term "firewall" comes from construction walls designed to contain fires, and the name stuck along with its depiction.

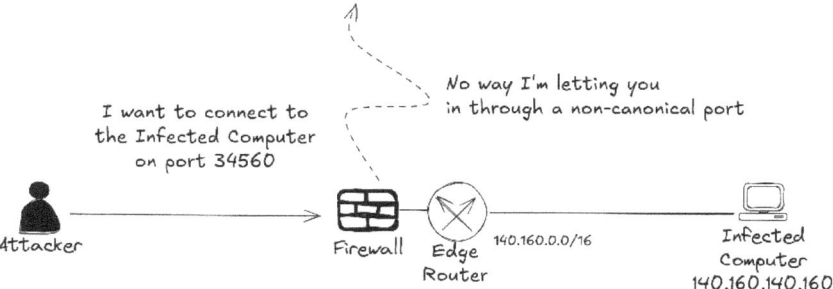

So, what are the priorities for setting up a proper firewall? At the scale of a small network like that of a home, firewalls are fairly simple yet still quite effective. For example, a default firewall may have the following settings:

Firewall Settings

allow all outgoing traffic ---→ **LAN-to-WAN: Allow all**

block only this incoming traffic ---→ **WAN-to-LAN: Block the following:**
                                                113

This basically means that all outgoing communications are allowed while incoming communications are blocked for port 113 (or the IDENT protocol). Why 113? Well, in the past, it was considered a good idea to ask computers about their owner. They would then reply with the owner of a connection, which would often be a system username. This is blocked because information asymmetry is part of a good strategy. It is also good to block this because an attacker who knows the system username may attempt to log in using that username, and even if they do not succeed, they may end up blocking access to the account. It's like letting a stranger know your middle name. I mean, sure, but why?

The above, of course, is just one configuration. Firewalls have several, including blocking many more ports than just 113. So let's look at a more aggressive firewall configuration.

Firewall Settings

highly restrictive for applications ---→ **LAN-to-WAN: Allow only:**
                              HTTP, DNS, Email, NTP, VPN, iTunes

WAN-to-LAN: Block all non-related traffic
                                             ↑
                                             this means traffic for which NAT has no record of leaving the network

In this example, all incoming traffic is blocked. The term "unrelated" just means anything for which NAT has no outgoing record. This way, your video call can still work. For outgoing connections, there are strict criteria. In fact, I would argue that the criteria are so strict that some applications are unlikely to work on this setup. On the upside, you may not be able to make Skype calls, but any malware in the network won't be able to either.

I should mention that firewalls can also adapt and automatically configure themselves. These are typically more advanced than what your ISP's edge router would provide.

But while bells and whistles are good, let's talk in simple terms. What configuration should you choose for your firewall? Well, there are two strategies: that of the micromanager and that of the risk-accepting folk (I made this up as a term, by the way). The micromanager would typically focus on fine-tuning every incoming and outgoing port. This generates a secure but dysfunctional network, and maintenance becomes costly. The risk-accepting folk would typically assign broader firewall rules that permit users a range of applications in the network, including some that the security engineer may not have intended. But that's okay since, with a good monitoring and incident response strategy, you can still address security events in the network while keeping the 3 a.m. calls to permit another port to a minimum.

Finally, network monitoring and firewalls work great together when they are positioned appropriately. Here's the correct configuration:

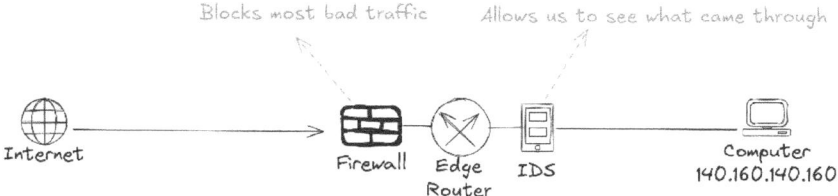

Notice that the firewall sits in front of the IDS in respect to the outside world. This makes sense since you wouldn't want to be observing traffic that has already been blocked by the firewall.

Evaluating ports to the outside world

Different networks may have additional devices at the edge of the network. This could be an email server or a web server. Edge devices are typically physically located near the edge, but that doesn't have to be the case. You can configure your edge router to route traffic to a computer deep inside your network. Therefore, your database, media server, or even a VPN might be located elsewhere in the network, rather than directly on your edge router. However, their ports are open to the outside world.

How? To bypass NAT, port forwarding is used to inform the router that a service runs on a computer within the internal network. For example, a web server running on ports 80 and 443 (TCP) would typically have port forwarding set up on an edge router that uses NAT so that traffic from the outside world can reach that machine.

With the advent of remote work, VPNs are also activated in networks, and access to these services is provided by either the edge router, if it is capable of doing so, or a secondary machine within the network. A port forwarding rule is then set up. For instance, OpenVPN uses port 1194 over UDP.

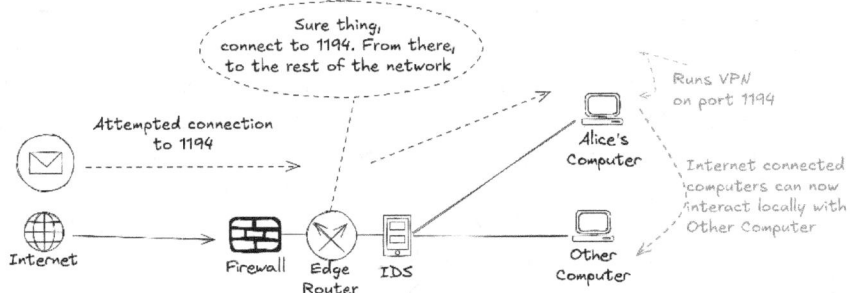

These open ports to the outside world are entry points. Think of your network as a fortress and the few gates as doors to the outside world. You need to keep an eye on them. You need to do the following:

- Identify all ports exposed to the world by inventorying, fingerprinting (i.e., examining the network data), or performing a port scan from outside your network.
- Once you know these ports, design graphs based on your network traffic and set up alerts for anomalies.

Naturally, you may ask, what should you be looking for? It depends largely on the protocol. For VPN access, you would want to determine the duration of valid connections versus invalid ones (hint: the invalid ones will have a duration of 0). Then, for valid connections, it would be good to know where they originated from. On the other hand, for web server or mail traffic, you would want to see primarily where incoming connections are coming from and how many requests or how much data volume you get for such connections. Basically, you are looking for spikes in traffic.

Observing inbound and outbound communications

One aspect of your perimeter, which is basically where your IDS is located, is to observe both the volume and frequency of inbound and outbound communications. There are a few things that you want to determine:

- How much is my daily volume, and does it match my daily

volume from similar past days?
- Which computers are communicating excessively, and with which other computers? Consider whitelisting the connections that are deemed safe and repeat.
- How much data are you sending to servers or clients?

The last one sounds a bit weird, so I need to elaborate. The two-tier architecture on the internet looks like this:

There is essentially a client that connects to the server. The initiator is always a client, and the recipient is a server. This is in respect to a connection, not a packet. You can determine which side of the communication ends is a server by looking at packets because they will usually have a low-numbered port. The client, in turn, will have a higher-numbered port. These are rough rules but work surprisingly well. By knowing which side is which, you can then establish the bytes sent to the server and the bytes returned to the client. NetFlow and IDS software do just that, but they do not use the ports to determine the client from the server. In the case of TCP traffic, it just looks for the TCP handshake.

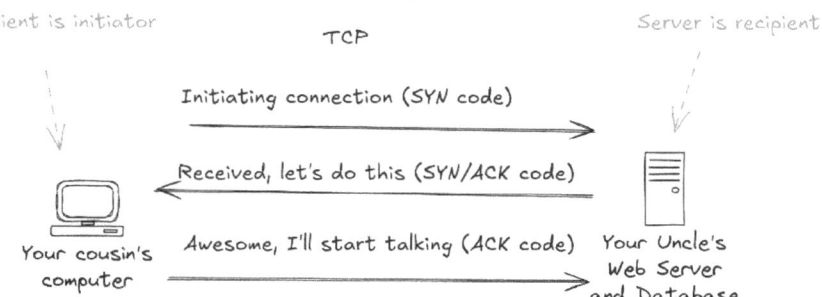

Every connection in TCP requires this three-step process, so the one initiating it is always the client. UDP is slightly different since the whole point of the protocol is real-time communication, and so its packets are unsolicited. However, if you observe network traffic for a while and suddenly see an outgoing packet via UDP to some destination, you can assume that the sender is the client and the destination is the server. Since UDP connections do not close gracefully like TCP connections, timers are used to determine when the communication has ended. Now that we understand the how, let's talk about the why. Let's imagine a user watching a movie over some stream.

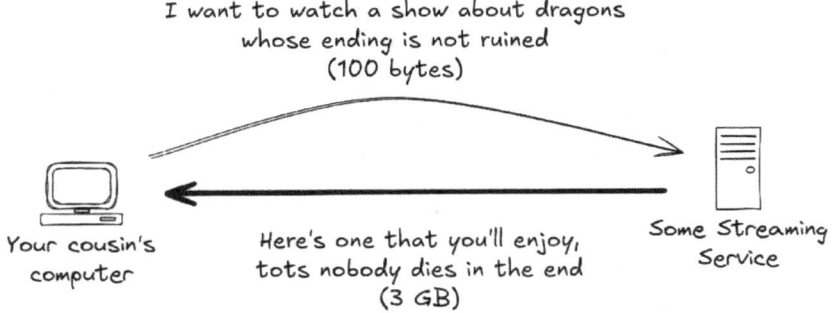

Notice that the user is receiving a lot of data. They have connected to a server and are now receiving the movie data as the client. This is a common pattern in most networks. The majority of traffic you will observe in a two-tier architecture involves people downloading data from servers. Web browsing exhibits similar behavior.

On the other hand, spikes in traffic to a server are rarely observed. These typically occur when you back up photos or other files. Video calls also require some uploading, but proportionally, there is much more downloading during the video call.

If I were to mirror the two traffic patterns for comparison, it would look something like this:

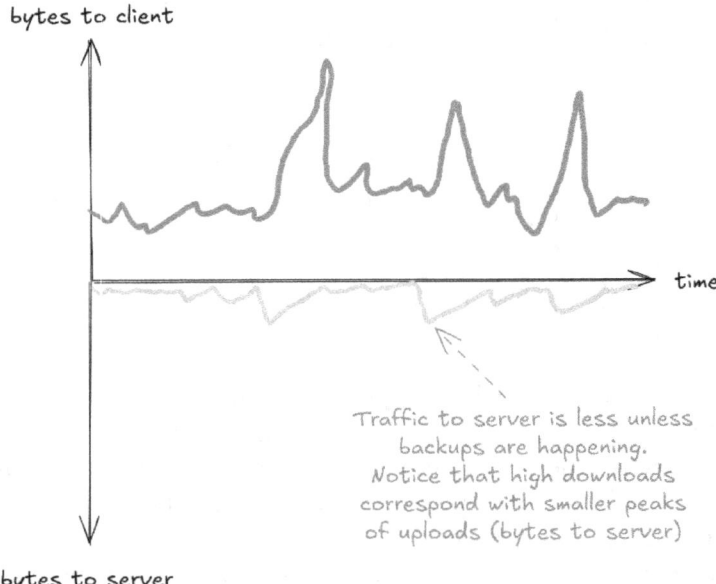

Notice that transmissions to a server are less than to a client. This still holds true even if you have a server on your network, such as a web server. Incoming connections from the outside world will still transmit very little data to the server.

If you observe a spike on this diagram in the "to server" traffic, what else, besides a backup, could it indicate? How about data theft? It happens quite often in networks, and now you have a tool that can help you identify it. So, keep an eye out for high "to server" traffic proportional to "to client" traffic.

Real-world example: Underperforming firewall

Network traffic is a fantastic tool that can help you determine whether you have an underperforming firewall. This happened once with my students observing a public network. There was a spike in incoming traffic through various ports. Just like with bytes to client and to server, often most NetFlow or IDS software tracks packets to client and to server. So what my students were seeing were incoming packets that had no packets to client (i.e., no response).

```
source IP: 1.1.1.1
destination IP: 192.168.0.1
    bytes to server: 100
        bytes to client: 0   <----- No response?
```

Whenever I have seen this pattern, my first instinct is to say that someone placed the IDS before the firewall. In other words, we were observing what would eventually be blocked by the firewall, hence the lack of response.

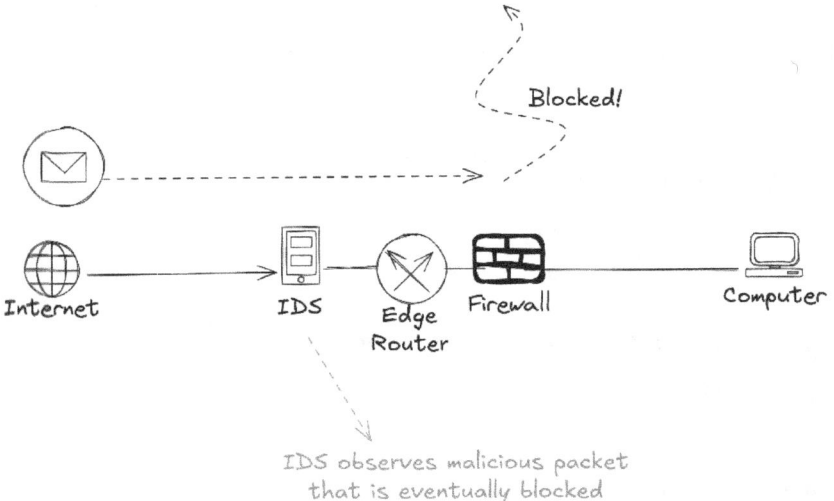

IDS observes malicious packet that is eventually blocked

I tasked my students with contrasting last week's observations, and, lo and behold, there was a difference. I also knew that they were unlikely to have moved the IDS. We ended up escalating the issue to the customer, and it turns out that a recent update to the firewall rules had misconfigured it in such a way that it allowed all sorts of traffic into the network.

As a result, incoming packets were effectively probing the network for various open ports. It didn't help that the internal network was not behind a NAT and computers were using public IPs.

Therefore, you need to look for connections that are one-sided, meaning zero packets or bytes to the client. These are indicative of something being off, and in this case, it was the firewall.

Real-world example: What does spam look like in networks

Kids like to build sandcastles only to eventually realize that they won't hold. I won't sugarcoat it for you: There is no way to stop spam completely, even if you are sold some AI dream software. Spam is email, in fact, one that attempts to look legitimate. That always leaves room for spam to get past spam filters.

What are spam filters? They are just a bunch of lexical and other behavioral rules regarding email data and metadata to determine whether something is likely to be spam.

The reality is that when observing network traffic, you will see spam right before your eyes. Mail traffic is encrypted, so instead, you end up seeing just a bunch of bytes delivered to a mail server. However, you can pay attention to patterns, especially regarding where something came from.

My students once spotted one such spike coming from a country with a particular reputation for that sort of thing.

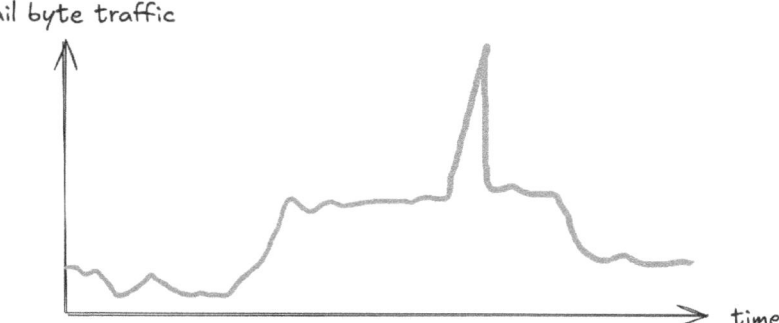

We quickly realized that this was a spam campaign targeting this particular customer. By measuring the volume of mail that came from a particular place in the world during a short time span, you can safely assume that there is an active spam campaign. Half of my students raised their hands and said we should do something, while the other half suggested raising the issue with the customer. Why? They quickly realized that it was a numbers game. Anyone, under the right circumstances, can fall victim to spam mail, and some spam emails can make it past a spam filter.

This combination means that a large spam campaign could be successful even in the most secure organizations. However, since we saw it happening, we notified them about it, and they raised it with their staff, who were more vigilant when they opened their mailboxes that day. So, if you have a mail server on a network, keep an eye on ports 25, 587, and 465 (all SMTP-related).

Summary

- Maintaining a tight perimeter is key to securing your network.
- Evaluating all open ports on your edge routers that are forwarded is key to understanding the potential points of entry (attack vectors) to your network.
- Firewalls are key to blocking unwanted traffic and should be frequently evaluated for misconfigurations.
- Keep an eye on traffic between clients and servers, as that will

reveal the directionality of byte transfers.

6 DETECTING DATA THEFT USING NETFLOW

- Learn some of the common ways through which data theft occurs.
- Discover common methods to identify them.
- Learn about data tunnels and exfiltration.

Overview

In today's digital world, data is incredibly valuable—it drives businesses, informs decisions, and connects us all. Unfortunately, it also attracts cybercriminals eager to steal sensitive information for financial gain or malicious intent. We've seen alarming incidents like the Equifax breach in 2017, where the personal details of 147 million people were exposed, or the 2018 Marriott International breach that compromised 500 million customers' data. These examples highlight just how serious data theft can be. This is where you come in and why understanding and using NetFlow for detection is crucial. NetFlow, a protocol developed by Cisco, gives you detailed insights into network traffic. It effectively aggregates information about a connection, telling you the source and destination IPs, the ports involved, and the number of packets and bytes transferred. By monitoring and analyzing this traffic, you can spot unusual activity, trace unauthorized access, and act quickly to protect your data.

Examining the avenues of data exfiltration

You may be asking, how is data stolen from networks? There are several ways that data theft happens, and some are not so obvious.

Attack vectors

Let's start with an easy one: phishing attacks. For these to work, an attacker needs to find an "in," or in technical terms, an attack vector. This can be an email, a message, or even a website. Through that, they can extract sensitive information from a victim, which is effectively data. By the way, money is also on the table, even though I am not focusing on this since this chapter is about data theft.

As an example, consider one of the earliest internet scams, the "Nigerian prince" scam. There are several variations of this, but the most mainstream involves an email from someone claiming to be a Nigerian prince from some tribe who has been trapped in [insert U.S. state or country] and needs you to transfer them some money with the promise of a handsome reward once they get back to Nigeria. In this case, the attack vector is your email.

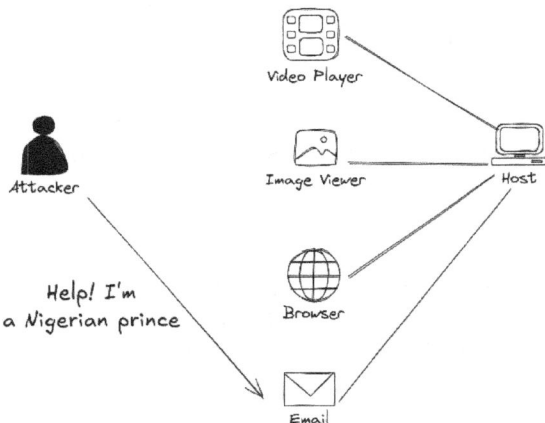

Email is also a great attack vector for the second approach that eventually leads to data theft: malware. This is a generic term used to describe *malicious software* (commonly referred to as a *virus*). Clicking on an attachment can infect a computer with malware designed to do various things, including stealing keystrokes from the user. For example, a user may often type their password on a website. The keystrokes become valuable data that, once they reach the attackers' hands, are extremely useful. Most malware will need to transmit such data through the network.

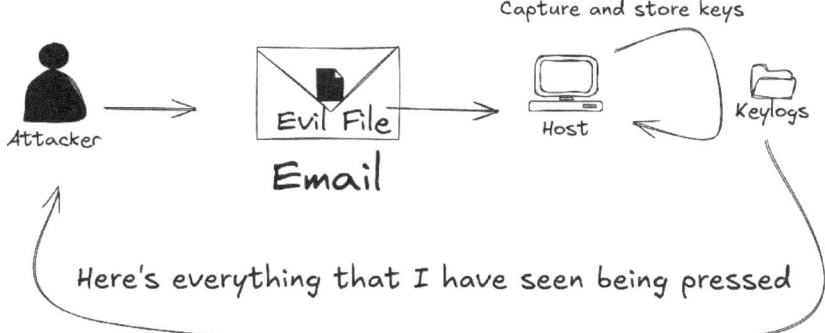

Ransomware works slightly differently. Its objective is to rapidly encrypt data on the disk and then extort the user for money with the promise of a decryption key. It is not stealthy (i.e., you'll know that you have it), and by the time it happens, there is not much you can do, even if you see evidence of network communication between an attacker and your computer.

An employee can also steal data from a network. We refer to this as an *insider threat*, the evidence of which may exist in the network or may occur out of band (i.e., through some other communication channel such as a USB stick). The likelihood of detecting this in time will vary depending on the approach, but given that the value of data is often measured in gigabytes, it can take a while to remove that data from a network.

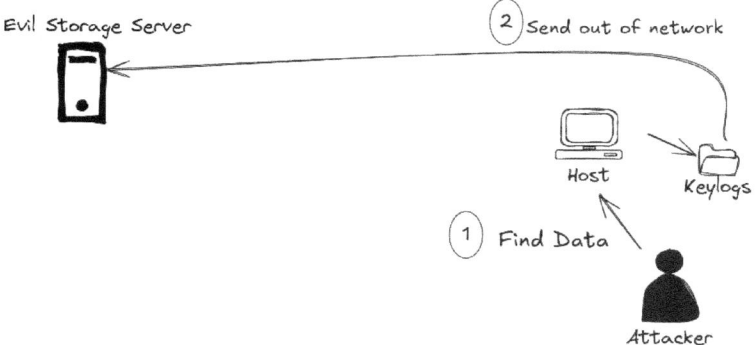

Another attack vector is identifying a weak cloud security point and exfiltrating data from that point. This is becoming increasingly common as many companies move their data storage to the cloud to save space (and money). In 2019, there was a breach at Capital One. The attacker found a misconfigured web application firewall that allowed them to access the cloud storage services on Amazon, where Capital One's data was stored. The ability to detect this through network security monitoring can be uncertain at best since it largely depends on the logging data these cloud providers provide. In other words, you can't just set up your own IDS in their network.

Paths for data exfiltration

Assuming that an attacker elects to remove data through your network (ideally the portion of the network that you are monitoring), you have a chance of detecting that exfiltration, but it is far from simple. They will likely attempt to mask their data exfiltration so that it appears as part of regular internet traffic.

The first way that data exfiltration might occur is via *Command and Control* (C2) channels. In the previous chapter, we discussed why most modern malware has C2 channels. This behavior is also how we can detect the presence of malware and exfiltration. For example, if you observe large data transfers to Australia and you are located in the United States, you would need to investigate this as a suspicious event in your network. You would evaluate the destination and determine who owns that IP address. Typically, it is an ISP, but it could also be a cloud service provider, a university, or a government organization.

Another interesting aspect of C2 communications is that they appear as regular traffic. It is not uncommon for such communications to occur under the HTTP protocol. In other words, it would appear as if you were connecting to a website somewhere. To make matters worse, traffic from most video streaming providers (e.g., Netflix) also uses HTTP, although you download data rather than sending it (more on that later).

However, attackers can be even more creative. For example, they could use the DNS protocol for data exfiltration. For this to work, they need to purchase a domain name and host their own DNS server for that domain. Then, when the malware wants to contact that domain name, your computer will use the regular DNS process to find out the IP address for that domain name. It looks like this:

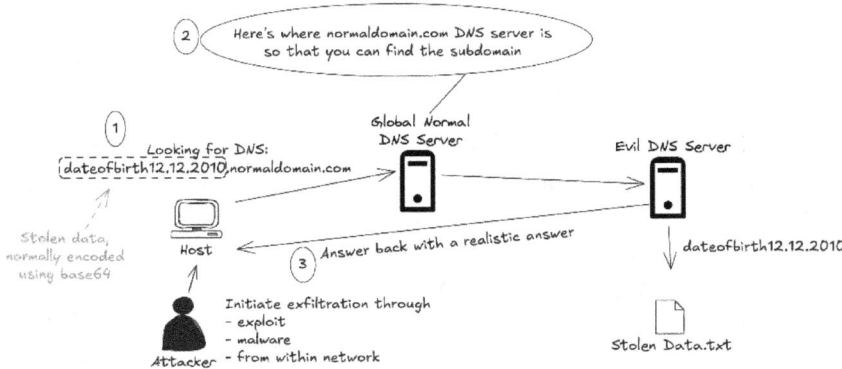

So what, you may say. Well, it turns out that domain names can also have subdomains. These subdomains can be quite large, and if someone were to use that space for sending out DNS requests, their own DNS server could receive and store these. For example, if I were to make a DNS request for thisisasecretmessage.evilserver.com, all I would need to do to get the first portion is to have my evilserver DNS server read and store the subdomain. The malware can keep making such DNS requests and slowly exfiltrate data out of a network.

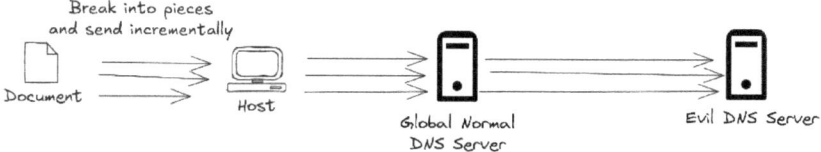

Does this work? Well, it worked for the attackers who exfiltrated data from Equifax. They used the DNS protocol over the course of 2 months to exfiltrate 150 million records of sensitive data. Why 2 months? Because, as we will see, DNS requests generate a lot of network noise. You just have to pay attention to your network to see them.

Evaluating what comes in and what goes out

So far, I have given you a few examples of how data exfiltration happens, but you may be wondering: what is the systemic approach for identifying such an incident? If you could ask an IDS in natural language to find out if there is data exfiltration in your network, you would say something like this: "Give me the sum of bytes transferred to external IP addresses per connection over various time frames."

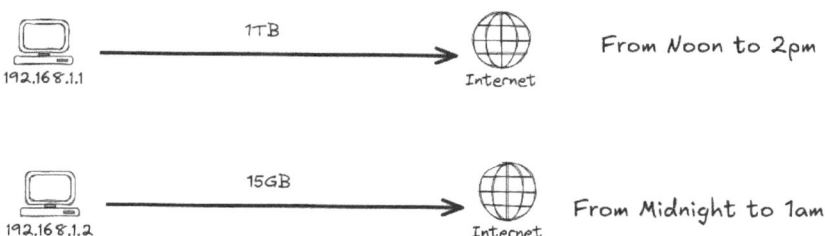

You are basically looking for data transfers to a server. Notice that I didn't say outgoing connections, because technically, when you stream video on YouTube, you have an outgoing connection to Google's servers. You are instead looking for the total bytes transferred from the server of that external IP. Let's look at a visual:

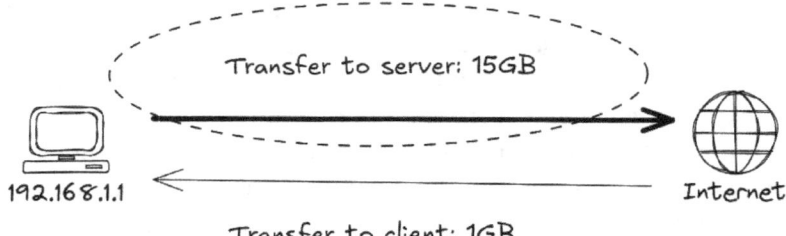

The circled portion represents the bytes going to a server. Whether that server has an external IP address or an internal one is less interesting. Visualizing this will require you to juxtapose byte transfers to clients with byte transfers to servers. Because the internet, and by extension network traffic, follow a producer-consumer model (i.e., servers have data, and people consume data from servers), you would expect to see an 80% to 20% ratio between transfers to clients and to servers, respectively. By the way, I made these percentages up. The real percentages will vary from network to network, but they will likely be consistent over time since people's habits do not change overnight.

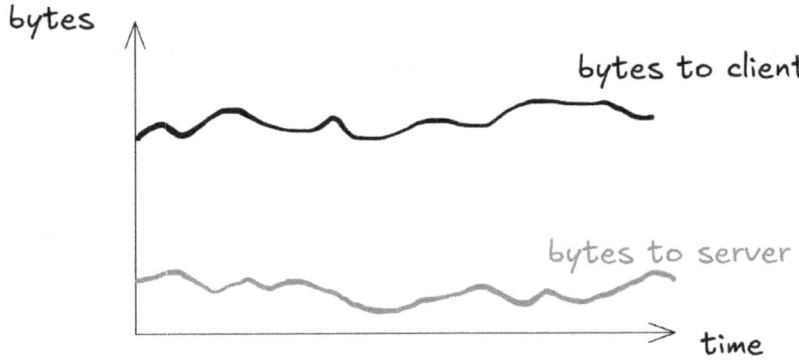

An anomaly is when we deviate from this normal trend.

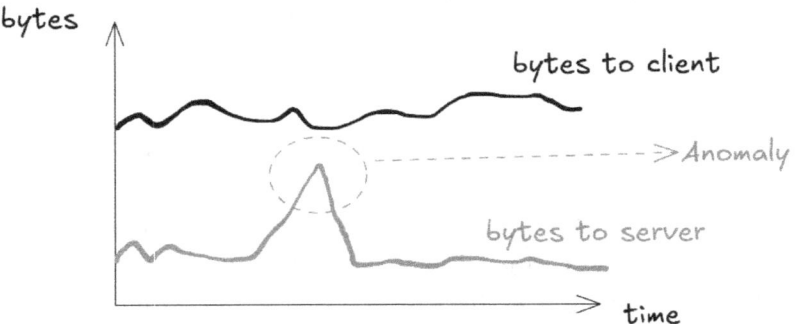

If you were to see the above, then you need to investigate why there was a large transfer to a server. The most common answer is "backups."

Many corporate networks have backups running, but you will also see such backups in your local network. When your photos are backed up from your phone to the cloud over your Wi-Fi, you will observe that trend. The second likely answer, if you observe such network traffic and it is not a backup, is that data exfiltration may be occurring.

A small caveat for this strategy does exist. If an attacker finds a wide-open web server and downloads records to their computer, then such traffic will appear similar to someone watching a YouTube video. In other words, byte transfers are directed toward a client in this case. This is a limitation of this approach, and in these cases, you will need to look for general byte transfers and compare whether these appear to be normal based on the context, such as whether this IP communicates with that one frequently and other similar questions. Such incidents happen less often since web servers are not as frequently exposed in the open web (otherwise breaches would be way more common). They can also occur in scenarios where an insider threat exists, and that is something we will discuss in a later chapter.

Detecting Exfiltration using NetFlow

NetFlow data are uniquely peculiar as data points for security analysis. Network packets are easy to understand; they are singular and have a certain size. NetFlow, on the other hand, is the aggregate of data over the time that a connection has remained active. This also reveals the first limitation: you won't see a NetFlow record until a connection terminates. Yes, you read that right. If a connection lasts for a month, you won't see the record for that connection until it terminates.

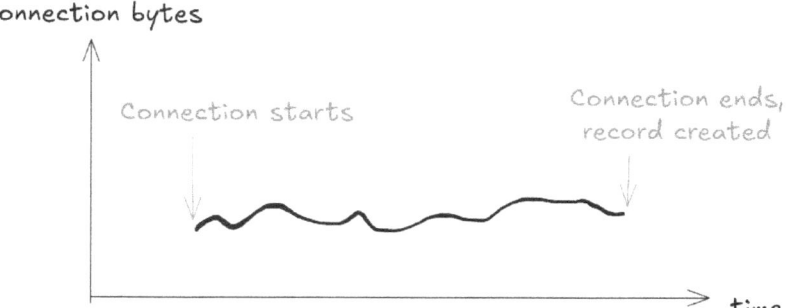

However, usually, most connections have a short lifespan (minutes at best) since they are designed to terminate and restart. HTTP traffic, for example, works that way. Each time a page refreshes on a website, a new connection (multiple, actually) is initiated.

The above is the case for TCP connections; however, with the advent of real-time communications, more and more the UDP protocol is used for data transfers. UDP does not have a connection-opening sequence (known as a three-way handshake) or a terminating sequence (known as a four-way handshake). Therefore, the IDS (or NetFlow collector) has to make some educated guesses on when a UDP connection is terminated. Usually, timers are used.

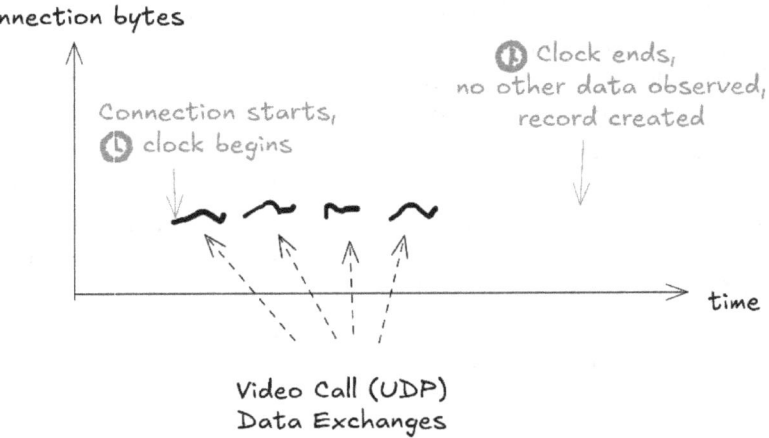

Video Call (UDP) Data Exchanges

However, this can be far from perfect given network congestion and other delays that may occur, so even if a real-time session lasts two hours, it may appear as two separate NetFlow hour-long records if there is a gap that lasts too long.

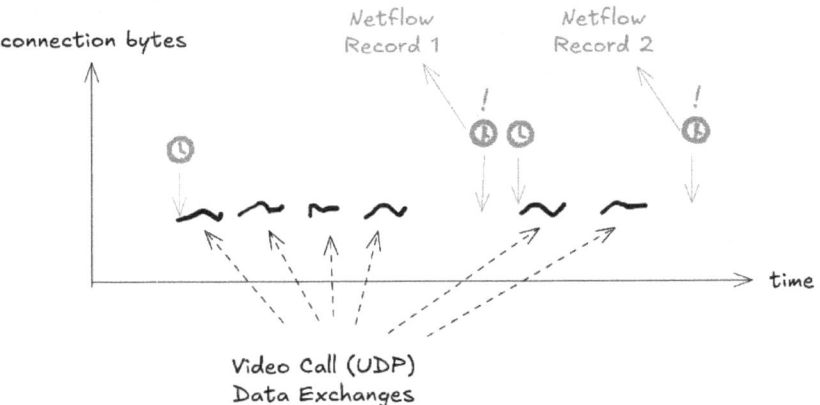

Video Call (UDP) Data Exchanges

Regardless, exfiltration in NetFlow means a lot of data, so you are likely to see a spike in total aggregate bytes.

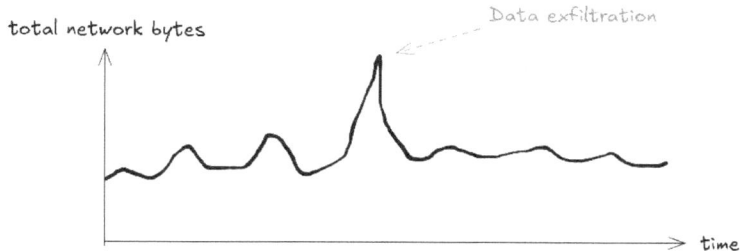

However, given that a single NetFlow record's byte count is relative to the time of the connection, you may want to often contextualize the byte transfer rate for each connection. In plain words, for each NetFlow record, you want to divide the total bytes transferred by the time the NetFlow connection remains open.

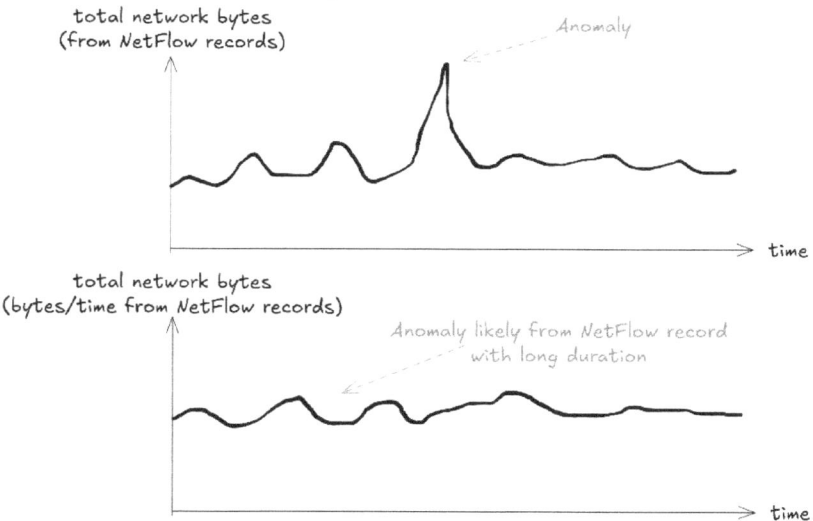

This means that a 10GB transfer over a week-long connection does not sound as impressive as a 10GB transfer over a minute. This is the unique aspect of analyzing network traffic using NetFlow; otherwise, bytes are bytes, and they represent the same thing as the files occupying space on the disk. If you notice large byte transfers on your network, you should follow up with an investigation.

Real-world example: DNS tunnels

Ever since the Equifax data theft happened spectacularly through DNS, I often tell my students that they need to pay attention to their DNS data transfers. There are two concepts to keep in mind: DNS tunnels and DNS exfiltration.

DNS tunnels are used to wrap network traffic through the DNS protocol. It works similarly to a regular VPN. In a VPN, you connect to an intermediary server that forwards your packets to the rest of the world, hiding the point of origin (assuming your browser or other applications don't leak your identity anyway). A DNS tunnel works similarly, except you need a domain name server and a domain.

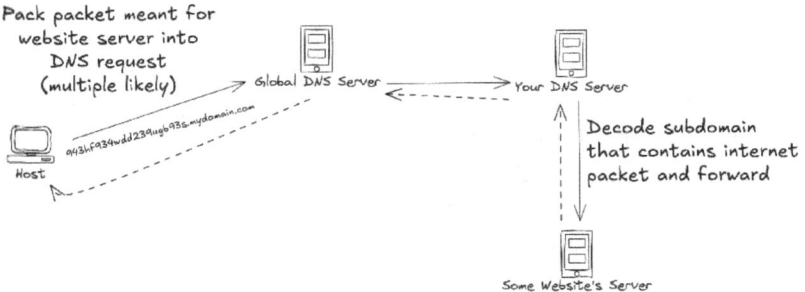

Data exfiltration is used specifically for extracting data. It is a DNS tunnel with a narrow purpose. The good news is that these activities are detectable by examining random-looking domain names and, in particular, subdomains.

jbswy3dpe.example.com
blw64tmmq.example.com

Given that moving data through the available character space (253 characters for domain and subdomain) is limiting, you can expect to see a lot of DNS requests. That means you don't even have to look for large byte transfers. The number of DNS requests in your network will skyrocket. For example, to exfiltrate 1 GB of data over DNS, you need about 4 million DNS requests.

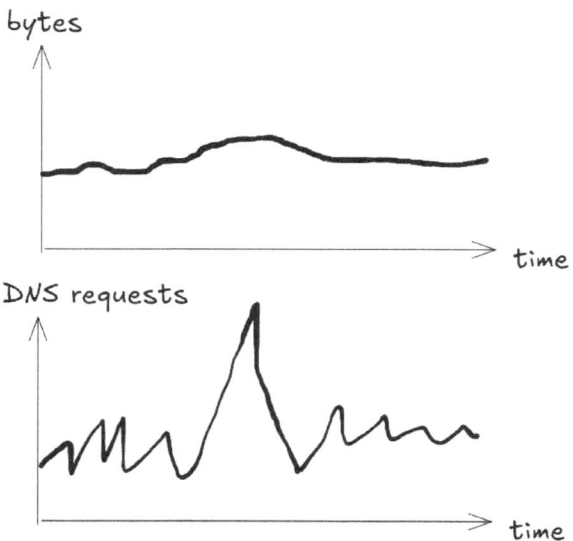

To be fair, even on NetFlow, you will be able to see the 1GB transfer, although it would not appear as impressive if you just looked at it across all protocols in the network. However, if you isolate only DNS traffic (port 53), then 1GB of transfer will still appear as a spike.

So, this is the point where I have some bad news for you. Hackers know that DNS exfiltration is highly visible, so they would avoid using it in nuclear mode (that is, really fast). They will instead introduce artificial delays so that the traffic can blend in with the regular traffic and transfer the data over a longer time window (think days).

Believe it or not, this is still detectable as long as you contextualize DNS requests per IP address in your network. Rarely would a computer produce 1GB worth of DNS traffic even over a month.

DNS Requests	IP
1,250,102	192.168.1.2
1,020	192.168.1.3
512	192.168.1.4
20,000	192.168.1.5

Anomaly! → (points to first row)

Real-world example: SSH theft using NetFlow

Some hackers who are less creative may choose to use other protocols to transfer data out of a network. One such example is using the Secure

Shell (SSH) protocol to transfer data. SSH is widely used across networks today to remotely manage Unix-based (e.g., Linux) computer systems via a terminal environment. For example, modern IDS usually run on Linux operating systems, and to configure them, people will need to connect via SSH remotely over port 22.

Turns out this protocol can also be used for file transfers. Cool, right? In fact, many backups and even IDS log data transfers to clusters are performed through SSH tunnels. In my classes, students often discover large data transfers over SSH and are worried about data theft. To this day, every single investigation of such large data transfers has been a backup. In other words, someone has a pre-programmed script backing up data from one computer to another over the network. This generates a lot of noise (sometimes even raising IDS alerts) and is detectable by simply looking at byte transfers, especially when contextualized over port 22. Here's how normal SSH traffic looks in my network for example.

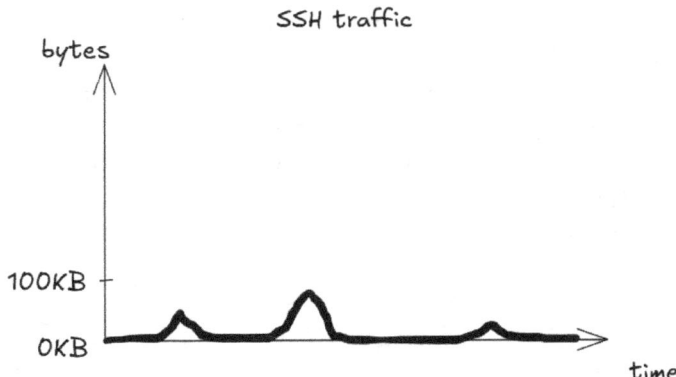

You can tell, it's usually peanuts. But you never know when there will be a case of actual data exfiltration over port 22. Ideally, never. By the way, this type of exfiltration is similar to DNS in the sense that the attacker knows that we can see it. One technique to bypass the fact that we can see it and also evade anomaly detection (more on that in a later chapter) is to use the boiling frog method (an awful name, but the industry understands it). The concept goes something like this: Since people are looking for large byte transfers, what if we had a way to determine regular data traffic over a network? Maybe it looks something like this:

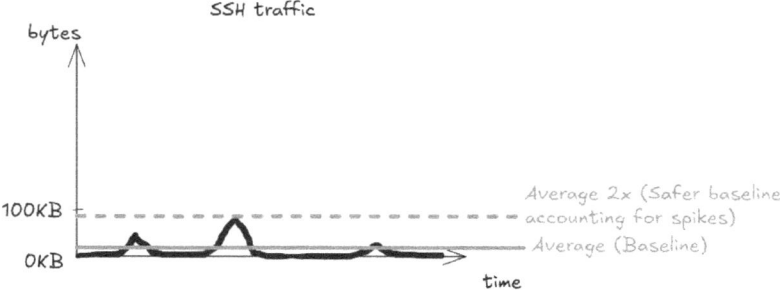

Then, just like a frog that doesn't realize it is being boiled alive, we can slowly turn up the heat. That is, start our data transfer slowly and gradually increase it. This effectively raises the baseline of data transfers in the network, and if done very slowly, we can gradually transmit data at higher rates without anyone realizing it.

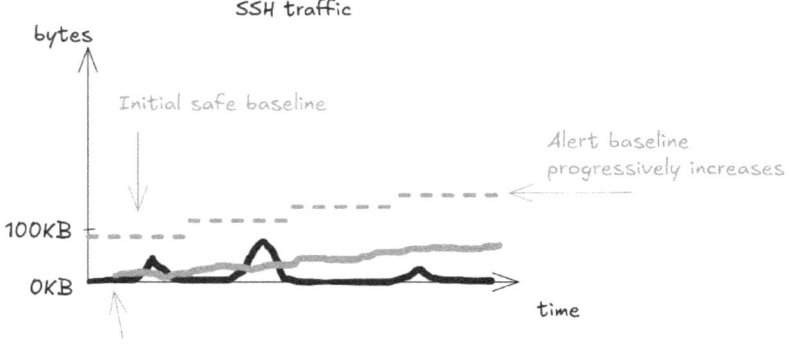

There is a way to tell if this has happened by conducting long-term analysis and comparing one week to another or one month to another. If there is a substantial difference in data transfers, then chances are something has fundamentally changed in the network. It could be data exfiltration, but it might not be. Either way, we have our eyes on the prize.

Summary

- Keeping an eye on data transfer spikes outside your network is key to determining malicious activity such data exfiltration or even C2 communications.
- Most data exfiltrations happen over regular network protocols, so you need to keep an eye on these for deviations from what's normal.

- DNS tunnels and related anomalies are easily detectable at looking at DNS requests. If these are encrypted, then frequency of requests would be a good indicator.
- SSH and HTTP tunnels and data exfiltrations can be detected by looking at the volume of data and for deviations from their baseline. The baseline is always relative to the network and the point in time that is observed.

7 HARNESSING INTRUSION DETECTION SYSTEMS

- Learn how to receive alerts through signatures.
- Identify critical alerts.
- Develop strategies to address false positive alerts.

Overview

So far, you have seen how you can use IDS to collect NetFlow data and use that data to inform you about the state of your network, as well as identify potential anomalies. However, IDS is primarily about deep packet inspection. This involves looking at the actual bytes and finding patterns that match predefined signatures. When these signatures match, they raise alerts, and then it is up to you to figure out what these alerts mean. Most alerts are benign, but some require your attention and action. This chapter will help you navigate through the challenging environment of IDS alerts. One final note: There are hundreds of thousands of IDS alerts, and you cannot possibly be expected to know all of them. What you need to be able to do is find out what each one means when you encounter it. Fortunately, the web is a great place for such information.

Understanding IDS alerts

I mentioned above that alerts are raised when signatures match certain packets. It is like having cargo ships pass in front of you in space while you scan them for contraband. In network terms, this may look like this:

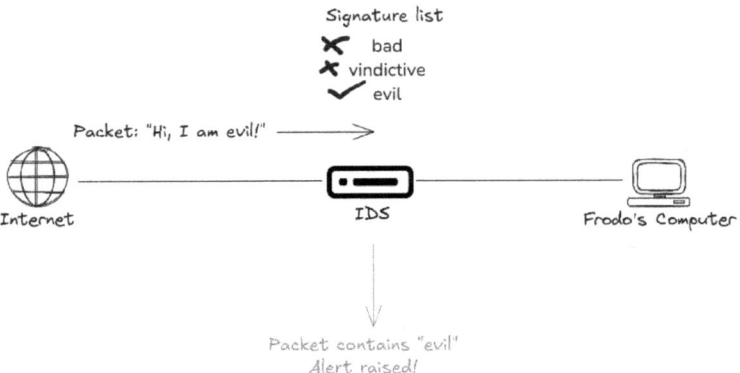

Some signatures may be a bit more complicated. They may necessitate the presence of a previous packet in order for a current packet to result in an alert. For example, if a camera detects movement inside a home, that would be an alert that depends on a single "packet." However, you can create a signature that triggers only if movement is detected and the door was previously found open. This means that an alert requires a sequence of events to occur.

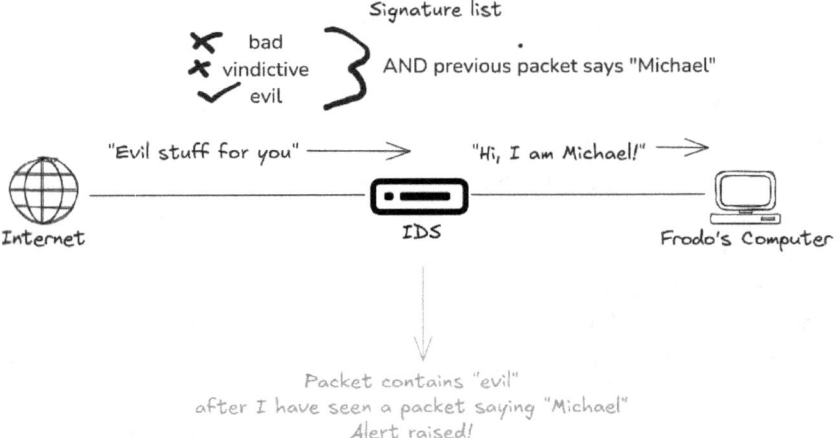

The complexity of these alerts can be dramatic. Some may search for a few bytes that match a signature on a TCP connection established under a specific port. The reason for this specificity is to reduce the number of false positives. Too many meaningless alerts will eventually lead to alert fatigue. Optimizing them makes them better, but even so, some alerts can only be optimized to a certain extent. Ultimately, you may still have an IDS that regularly produces a number of common false positives due to the circumstances in your network. Here's some in plain English just to give you an idea:

> *Malformed packet*
> *This computer didn't respond properly*
> *Some USB metadata from a computer*
> *Someone is using Messenger*

Due to the high number of false positives, we often refer to IDS alerts as Indicators of Compromise (IOC). Actually, IOC is a broader category that includes various elements such as Windows events and other items of interest that, as the name suggests, indicate something might be wrong, but we cannot be entirely sure. So, in the literature, you may see IOC used to describe IDS alerts as well. Regardless, their false-positive design is there for a reason.

For example, in one of the networks that my students were monitoring for a customer, a peer-to-peer alert for the eDonkey network kept appearing every minute. This network is similar to torrent networks or, for much older readers, networks like Napster. Essentially, you download files from other peer computers instead of a server, which is a counter-paradigm to the client-server architecture that we've discussed. As a side note, even peer-to-peer networks require the use of a server, so they are not entirely independent of the client-server architecture.

Anyway, we eventually discovered that the city had an HDMI-over-Ethernet device that was generating these alerts. We made a note to ignore it. It feels like an uncomfortable decision, given that these alerts are meant to detect malware and similar threats, but this is the nature of security analysis—a fine balance between sanity and insanity.

Common network alerts

There are some alerts that I tend to see frequently, and I'd like to save you some time. These alerts are common, though their names may vary depending on the IDS you're using. I will be using Suricata's (an IDS) alert names, but you are likely to find these alert names modified yet similar in other IDS. After all, the packets are the same, so the alert is raised for the same reason.

Diagnostic alerts

The first category of alerts relates to diagnostic network errors. These are often specific, such as ICMP errors or malformed packet headers. Here's some real alerts that come prepackaged with the IDS Suricata:

- GPL ICMP undefined code
- GPL ICMP Time-To-Live Exceeded in Transit undefined code
- GPL ICMP Echo Reply undefined code

These types of alerts can, more often than not, be safely ignored. In fact, I cannot recall a time when such an alert and its subsequent investigation resulted in a useful detection. They can inform you about the state of things in your network, such as whether there are devices that are misconfigured or have peculiar firmware, but deriving security concerns from that is unlikely.

STUN / NAT Traversal

The next category of alerts is informational. These do not often come pre-packaged with the IDS, but their signatures (or rules) are added into the IDS. They are maintained by a community (e.g., Emerging Threats), change with the times, and track popular software rather than network protocols. An example of this is "Session Traversal Utilities for NAT" or "STUN Binding." These are generated by software that attempts to bypass NAT so that communication can occur between the internal network and the outside world. It is popularly used by software such as Skype, Messenger, and most Voice over IP (VoIP) software (i.e., Internet Telephony).

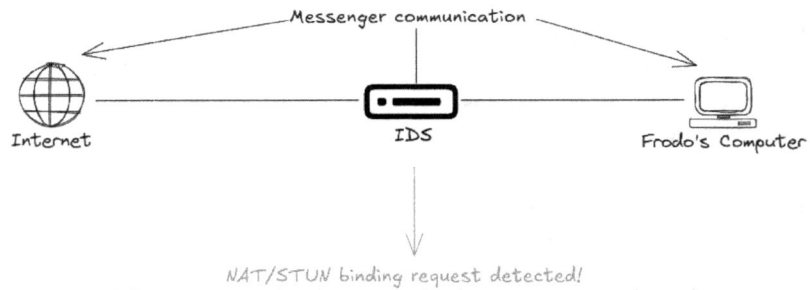

Are these worrisome? Well, it depends. In security analysis, especially when it comes to alerts, context is everything. If you are getting these alerts from a bunch of laptops that people use, and your workplace allows the use of messaging applications, then these alerts are normal. Or, if you want to call them false positives, that's also okay. On the other hand, if you have a computer that runs a database server and you suddenly observe these alerts, then you have to wonder why and investigate further by checking what else is running on that computer directly. This often means you need to physically check the machine's applications.

Heartbeat alerts

In a more direct vein, there are a series of alerts that detect various events from applications. Typically, these are heartbeat events. Applications need to report to servers that they are online, so they periodically send data out. There are such connectivity alerts for Android devices, as well as for software like Dropbox or Discord, to name a few. Should you be worried about these? It depends on the context. Are you running Discord on your machines? Does your organization permit its use?

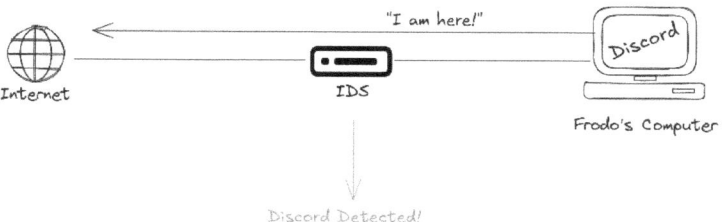

Public IP lookup

Moving on to more interesting things. Remember that modern computer networks sit behind routers that use NAT, creating an inner subnet of private IP addresses while the outside world operates with public IP addresses? Well, a lot of software is aware of this and needs to know what your computer's public IP address is, as opposed to its private one. Your public IP address is often shared among multiple computers, but that doesn't matter. By knowing your public IP, a remote computer can attempt to communicate with your network (whether it reaches your computer depends on whether ports are open) or at least determine your approximate location.

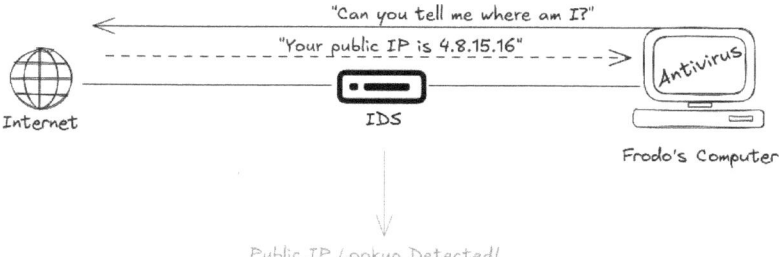

Lots of software does this, including antivirus programs. After all, companies need to collect marketing data on their customers. It turns out malware also needs to know what computer it has infected. The maker of malware does not always know where it will end up, so it is useful to find out. In the case of malware, it will typically ask an external server (often a legitimate service like ipify.org) to tell it its public IP address. Then, it will contact its C2 server to report the location of the infected computer and await further instructions.

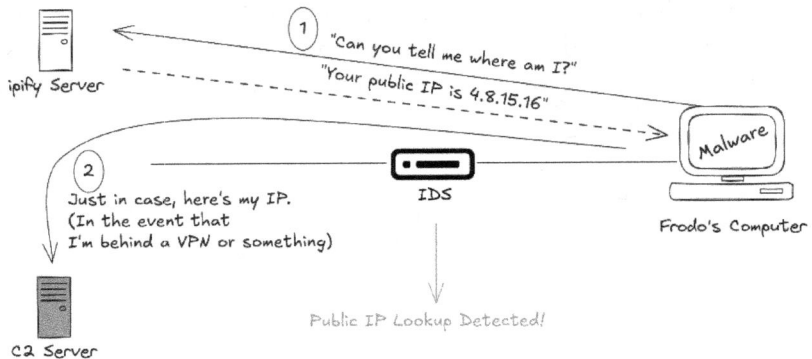

Dynamic DNS is another category that makes use of public IP lookups. This is for people who want to have a domain name (e.g., example.com) but do not have a reserved public IP to assign to their server. Instead, they make use of the ephemeral public IP assigned to them by their ISP. This IP can change, so Dynamic DNS updates the record whenever that happens by utilizing public IP lookups.

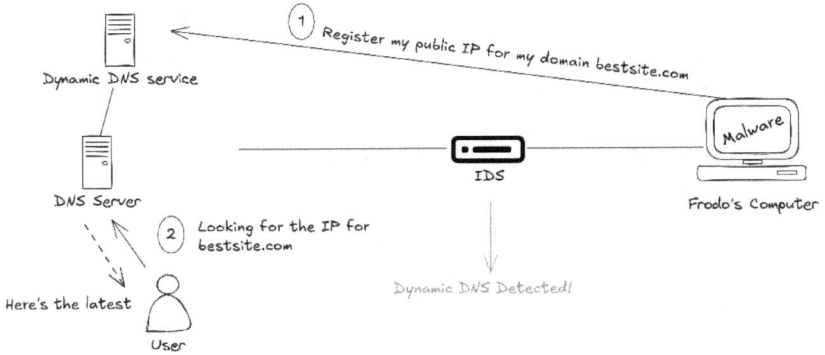

So, if you see this, ask the question: "What application wants to know my public IP address and why?" Often, it's benign, but you never know.

DNS over HTTPS

Here's a policy-type alert: DNS over HTTPS detection. I've already spoken about regular DNS used for resolving domain names. If you need to access google.com, what's its IP? Send a DNS request to a DNS server (e.g., Cloudflare's DNS is 1.1.1.1) and get back an IP address as a response. Side note: usually, DNS responses contain multiple addresses. DNS over HTTPS means sending these requests over an HTTPS channel. It's like wrapping it in wax paper to keep it secure.

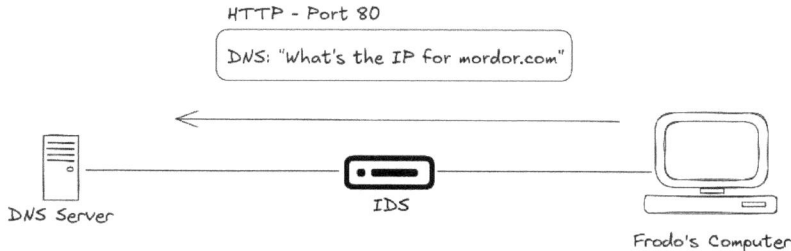

The good news is that the HTTPS channel is encrypted. Privacy benefits from this, but on the other hand, security analysis is slightly compromised. The alert essentially notifies you that someone is using DNS over HTTPS. Whether this is permissible depends on policy. However, there is something you can always do: check at least the HTTPS server used for this request. It should be a legitimate one, and if it is not, you will need to investigate further to determine the origin of the DNS request, specifically the software that made the request.

Exposed credentials

Speaking of policy alerts, exposed password credentials via HTTP is another unfortunately common alert. It means that someone accessed a website over HTTP (i.e., unencrypted) and then entered their password. Anyone eavesdropping along the line of communication could potentially have grabbed the password.

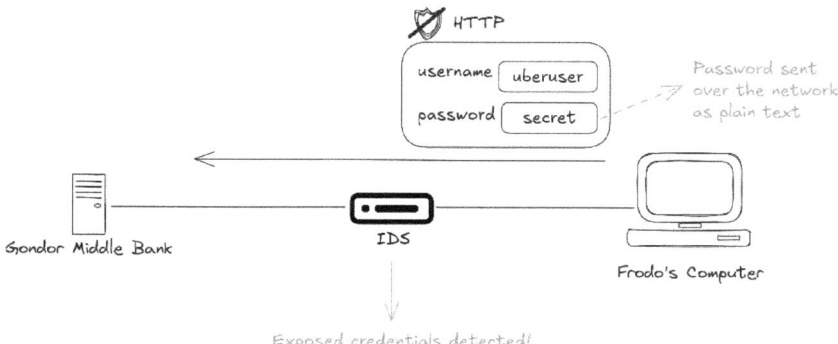

The password is considered compromised, so the unfortunate individual needs to be notified about the incident, trained to use HTTPS, and have their password changed. A slight exception to this is when the incident occurs in development environments inside private networks. In such cases, you can dig deep into your risk acceptance reserves and determine whether you need to take any action regarding the alert or incident.

Top domain alerts

There are also alerts about specific domains, top domains to be exact. These include ".tk," ".top," and ".cc." To be fair, the severity among these is far from equal, but these are basically domains whose providers have historically been lenient with tech scammers willing to use their domains. So, when a DNS request is observed for lotsofmoney.tk, the IDS picks this up and an alert is raised.

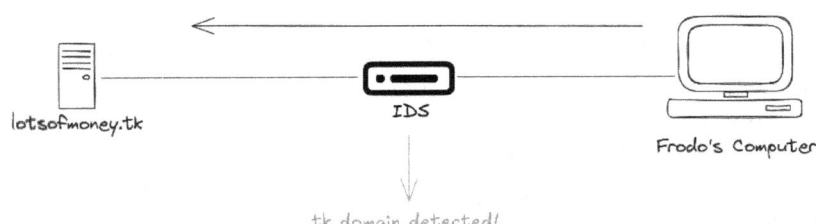

You should worry about these. They have been known to have exploits for browsers, phishing scams, or be used by malware as a means to communicate with their C2 (more on that in a later chapter). The domain .tk has an interesting and long history. It aimed to provide free domain names for people who could not afford them. They made money by showing ads on the websites as pop-ups. The island of Tokelau benefited from this model, and a large portion of its GDP depended on the domain name business. However, with that came the abuse of the domain space since there was little accountability for people receiving free domains. There was no paper trail between the registry and the domain registrant. Here's some good news, though: Freenom, the company associated with .tk and .cc domain names, exited the domain market in 2024. But because I'm a Debby Downer, I will say that the story is probably bound to repeat itself. Hackers appear to prefer specific domains for scams, so with the closure of these domains, others are likely to become popular, whether they are paid domains or free.

Malware alerts

In the unlikely event that you see an alert saying "malware" or "trojan horse," or something dramatic like that, you need to investigate immediately. From personal experience, these occur much less frequently than any of the previously mentioned alerts. However, the likelihood of them being false positives still exists. In fact, even if they are true, it doesn't necessarily mean that the malware's attempted exploit was successful. Some malware looks for weak, unpatched systems, and even if these do not exist, an alert can still be raised by the IDS because the exploitative packet is observed.

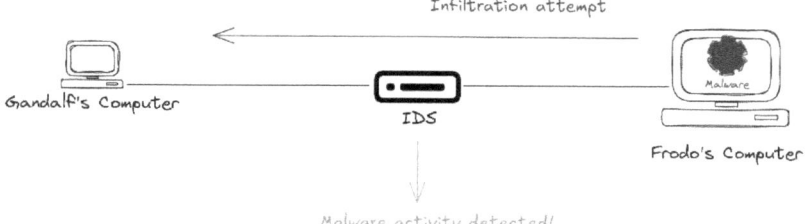

By the way, the above won't work if the packet doesn't pass through an IDS. For smaller networks, whose IDS is often placed at the edge of the network, internal communications can often be missed, such as the probing observed above by the malware. That's why the placement of IDS in the network (if you can place more than one, even better) is critical.

But either way, heed the alert's warning and investigate what caused it. You may just save your network.

Analyzing and responding to intrusions

Getting alerts and recognizing their degree of importance is necessary, but you'll also need to respond to them or at least understand some aspects of how responses work in larger teams. I'll simplify things to some degree.

So, say you observe an alert that you haven't seen before. What's next?

Step 1: Understanding the alert

You can often tell by the alert message, but if not, you need to understand what triggers the alert. Some alerts are triggered very easily. For example, say you are looking for a sequence of bytes: 73 70 61 6D (this spells "spam" in ASCII, by the way). The notation I used is in hexadecimal form (0 to 9 and A to F). Each byte consists of a pair of hexadecimal digits. So, in this case, we are looking for these 4 bytes in sequence. How likely is it that such a sequence will be observed randomly? You may be inclined to say it's not likely, but consider encrypted traffic, which appears as a random sequence of bytes since it's encrypted. If you observe 1,000,000 packets of 1MB each, the chances that one contains this sequence are not unlikely. If you run this through a binomial probability calculation, the likelihood of seeing this sequence anywhere in a packet at least once is a bit over 20%.

Sometimes alerts are also accompanied by references. These do not always appear in the analyst interface (e.g., Kibana), but you can find them in signatures. For example, here's a Suricata signature:

```
alert http any any -> any any (msg: "ET MALWARE [ANY.RUN]
Socks5Systemz HTTP C2 Connection";flow: established, to_server;
http.method; content: "GET"; http.uri; content: ".php?c="; pcre:
"/^((?:[a-f0-9]){2})+$/R"; http.user_agent; content: "Mozilla/5.0
(Windows|3b| U|3b| MSIE 9.0|3b| Windows NT 9.0|3b| en-US)"; bsize:
57; http.header_names; content: "|0d 0a|Host|0d 0a|User-Agent|0d 0a
0d 0a|"; reference: md5,545519a4f5847b77094b2a6baa5d1cfe;
reference: url,app.any.run/tasks/351c3d1b-05d6-483e-9480-
b4db71a8a9ff; classtype: command-and-control; sid: 1; rev: 1;)
```

It can be challenging to understand the above if you are not trained to read these. I highlighted the references. One contains a hash that identifies the malware. The other is a URL that references an analysis. Sometimes this information can be outdated, not working, or not useful. If all else fails, you can also use tools like ChatGPT to make sense of what this signature does. For example, I wrote to ChatGPT:

```
Explain to me the following signature and how likely it is to occur
in a random set of 1 million packets of 1MB size.

[Signature pasted below]
```

The answer I received is too large to paste here, but it did tell me that it looks for a specific HTTP header that contains a particular User Agent (this is the identifier typically used for browsers) and that it also looks for a specific packet size of 57 bytes. Thus, it's unlikely to trigger an alert among the million packets I mentioned, each being 1MB long. Who said generative AI cannot jest? Anyway, at least we know this is a highly specific alert, so if we observe it, it means it happened through HTTP, which can often be the result of a browser (although malware can use the protocol too).

Step 2: Understanding the players involved

You need to determine the IPs (i.e., computers) involved in the incident and the ports that were used. Was this a Local Area Network (LAN) only communication? In other words, is the source IP and destination IP within a private subnet (or a public subnet used behind a firewall, which is a bit more advanced of a discussion for another day)?

If the communication is local, you have to determine what the computers are used for. This involves IP fingerprinting, similar to the network fingerprinting described in Chapter 5 but for a single IP. Are they laptops or servers? Do they access the network via Wi-Fi or Ethernet? This will add necessary context. Some alerts are benign for laptops (e.g., messaging app alerts) but not for servers.

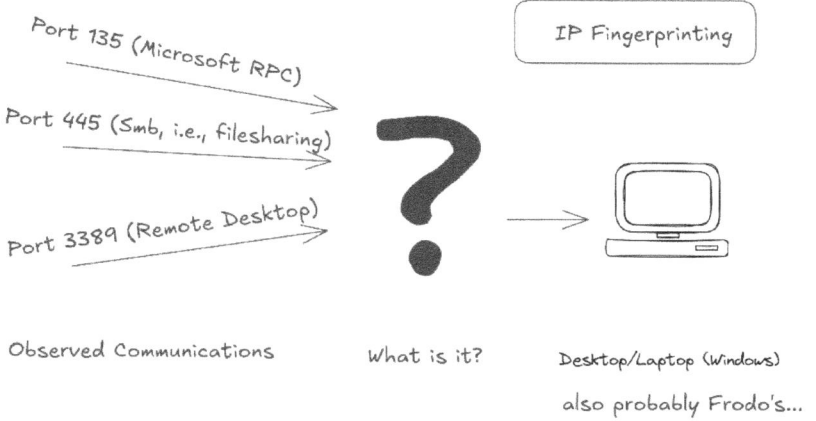

If the communication is between a Local Area Network (LAN) and a Wide Area Network (WAN), you need to further determine the reputation of the external IP. You can use various reputation lists that also provide geographic information about the IP (e.g., talosintelligence.com). The severity differs if the IP is not reported by any other sources as bad. The owner of the network (also known as the Autonomous System owner) is also key information that can help you better understand the nature of the foreign IP.

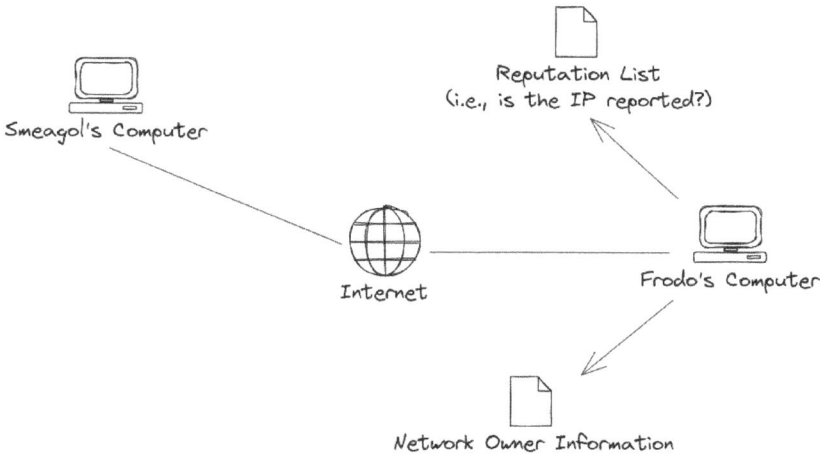

Then, you need to examine the ports used and determine the direction of the communication. Specifically:
- Who initiated the communication channel?
- What was the direction of the packet when the alert was raised?

The first question is easier to answer for TCP than for UDP, but the typical rule of thumb is that the lower port is the destination port. Typically, one side's port will be below 20,000 (well below that, actually), while the other side will have a port above 30,000 or 40,000, depending on the operating system. Just be careful when inspecting the alert's source and destination ports, as these do not always correspond to the direction of the communication channel. Here's an example that illustrates this:

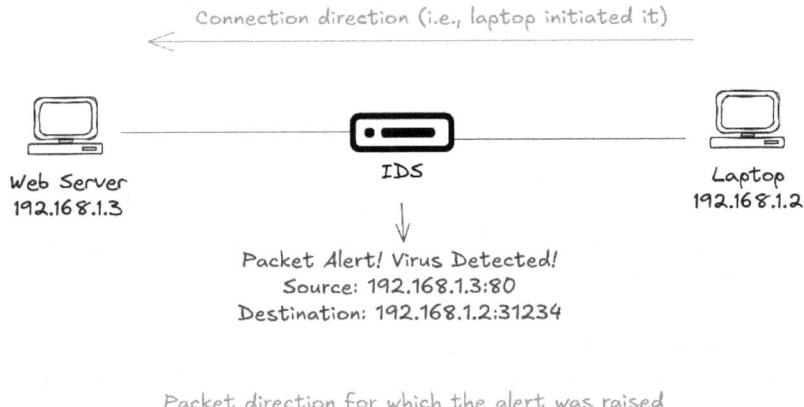

The directionality of the packet is what is stated in the alert, so it is easier to determine. Basically, you are trying to answer whether a computer reached out to the internet and if a computer on the internet attempted to send something peculiar to it, or vice versa, or any other combination for that matter. Context matters.

Step 3: Frequency of occurrence

You'll also need to determine the frequency of occurrence for the alert. Does it happen consistently at regular intervals, or in a non-deterministic (i.e., random) manner?

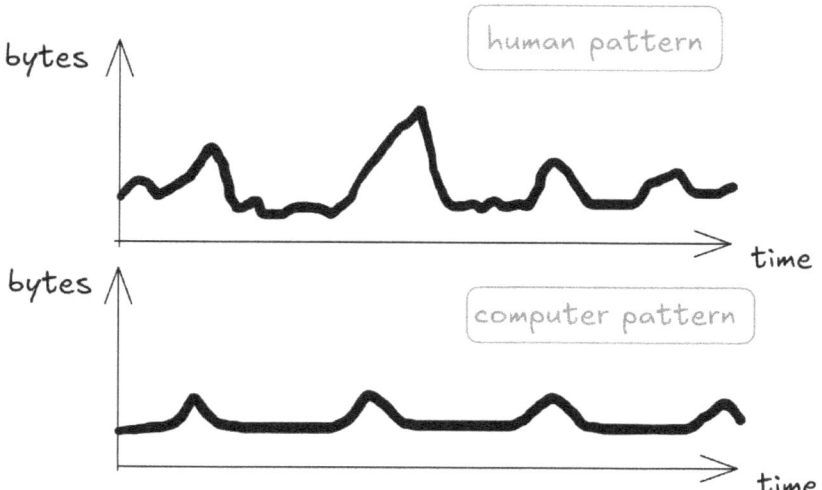

This can often tell you whether something is triggered by a human action or by a program (e.g., malware). I should mention that the above is a bit exaggerated. The difference is usually more nuanced but to a trained eye there is still a difference.

Step 4: Chain of events

You need to look beyond the alert at all other data available to you. For example, if NetFlow is captured, you will need to use it to determine, within the time window that the alert was raised, what else was happening on the local machine (or both local machines if that's the case). By "time window," we often mean a minute or two around the incident, typically a bit before and after. Sometimes there are events that happen that lead to an alert, so it is useful to know what these events are.

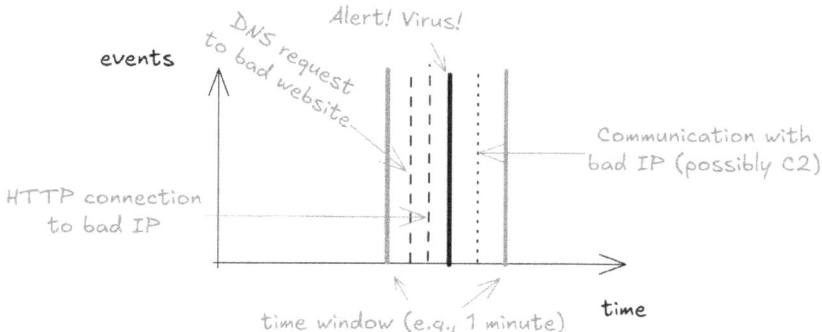

As a reminder, NetFlow is a record that spans a duration, while an alert occurs at a specific time. Therefore, when analyzing, make sure to use NetFlow's start and end times to look only at relevant NetFlows within the time window when the alert occurred.

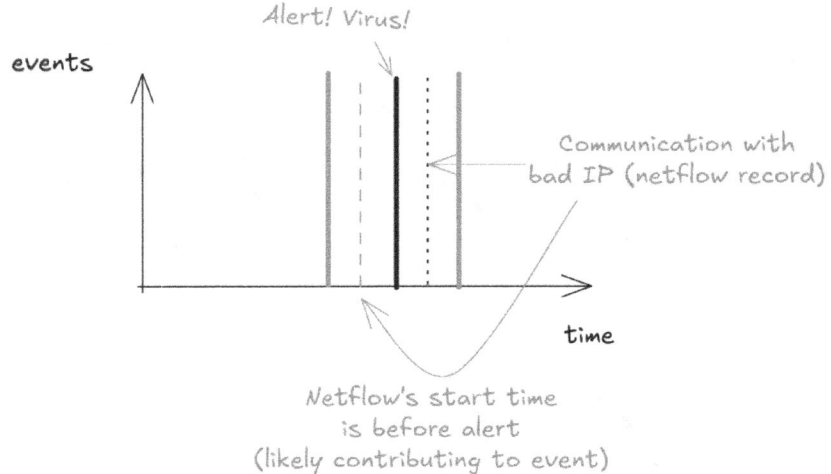

DNS requests can also be extremely helpful since they can reveal any domains requested before an incident occurs. For example, if there is a DNS request for gmail.com followed by an alert a minute later about a Trojan horse (i.e., a type of malware), it is possible that the Trojan horse originated from a phishing email.

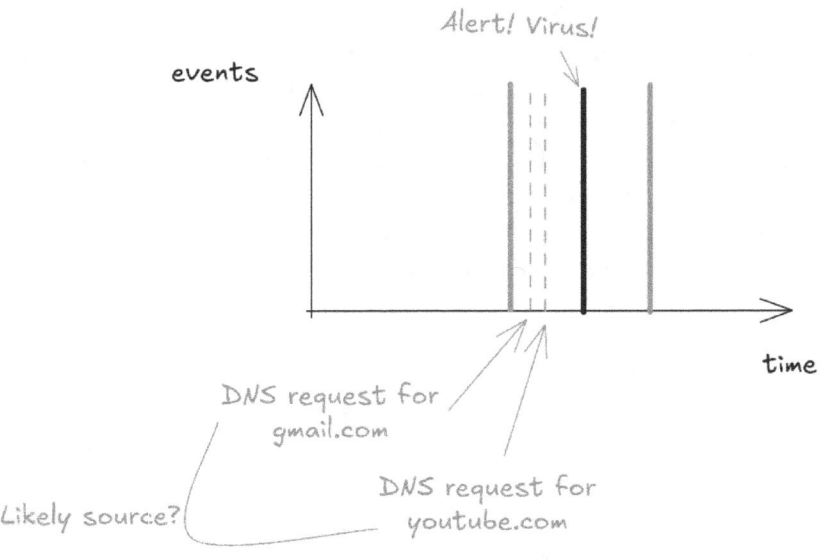

As a final note, you can never be 100% certain about a chain of events. Even if you had access to full packet captures, there is encryption, VPN traffic, DNS over HTTPS, and all other factors that could complicate network analysis. However, anything that moves the probability away from a coin toss (i.e., 50%) represents a positive analysis outcome.

Real-life example: Bitcoin mining

One of the strangest tickets that student analysts have ever encountered was related to Bitcoin mining. One day, without prior warning, an alert popped up: ET POLICY BitCoin User-Agent Likely Bitcoin Miner. I'll walk you through the steps described previously and provide you with the story behind it.

The first step was to determine what the alert was about. Google search or ChatGPT could work, but in this case, most of my students were familiar with Bitcoin mining. It is software that mines Bitcoin with the promise of paying you off eventually. We still needed to determine what the alert was about. If you search the alert using some Suricata syntax (e.g., "content:") or include "github.com" in your query, you might get lucky and find information about the actual rule.

```
alert http $HOME_NET any -> $EXTERNAL_NET any (msg:"ET POLICY BitCoin
User-Agent Likely Bitcoin Miner"; flow:established,to_server;
content:"BitCoin"; nocase; http_user_agent; fast_pattern:only;
reference:url,isc.sans.edu/diary.html?storyid=11059;
classtype:trojan-activity; sid:2013457; rev:4;)
```

It looks for outgoing (outbound) HTTP packets that contain the keyword "Bitcoin" anywhere. So, if I were to visit a website that talked about Bitcoin, it could trigger this alert. The trick is that HTTP is used and not HTTPS, which would be encrypted and therefore impossible for the IDS to read the content. Digging more on Google, they quickly discovered that Bitcoin mining does not require a lot of network byte transfers. Most of the mining occurs locally, and only parameters for solving each puzzle (the "mining" part) are exchanged.

The first thought that students had was that if it wasn't a false positive, it must be malware. This quickly changed in step two, determining the players involved. The outgoing packets that triggered the alert had a common destination, but the source IPs were different (i.e., multiple local computers were firing off these alerts). Well, malware could still be at play if a bunch of computers were infected. There were two ports involved, one of which was HTTP, which makes sense because of the alert, but there was another non-canonical port that also raised alerts.

The next step was to establish the frequency of occurrence. Before I show you what we saw, you can attempt to imagine what malware infecting multiple computers should look like. That would be constant mining from each infected computer while they are on. Some may be powered off at night while others are not, but the persistent effect when they are on should be there. There is malware that tries to do this in a stealthy manner by reducing its load on the system, but that would be a more advanced problem to solve.

Anyway, the graph looked something like this:

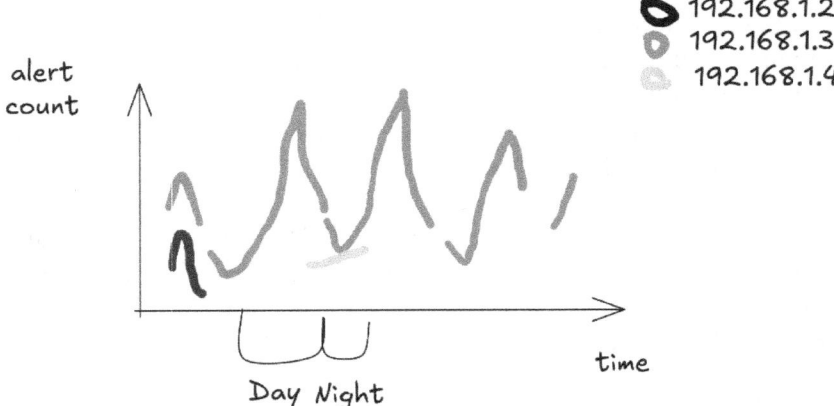

Actually, it's different since I cannot show you real data, but you get the idea. Multiple computers are on and off, running for a while and then stopping, while there is a strong preference for one computer that is always on. Notice that the frequency is also variable. Malware would try to maximize its time and not arbitrarily stop and start mining. So this started to look a lot more like a human. Our final step was to discover how, which is more difficult to do just by looking at data. Not all bitcoin mining software advertises its presence on the network, but in this case, we narrowed down the start and end points of activity right before an alert and analyzed the DNS queries. One of them was to a website that was known to be used via the browser for bitcoin mining. Armed with all the data, we delivered our report to the customer, and off it vanished into the annals of history, never to reveal to us the fate that awaited it. This is also a common thread for a security analyst, or so I hear. Don't expect to be paraded around like a superstar. There is also a certain sense of irony for the employee who performed such mining. Mining through a browser is ridiculously ineffective and unlikely to make any profit.

Real-life example: USB metadata

My students often see the following alert: ET INFO Windows OS Submitting USB Metadata to Microsoft. It's basically Windows sending metadata about a USB device that is inserted into a computer. Digging through Google, you can find the actual alert rule:

```
alert tcp $HOME_NET any -> $EXTERNAL_NET $HTTP_PORTS (msg:"ET INFO Windows OS Submitting USB Metadata to Microsoft";
```

```
flow:established,to_server; content:"POST"; http_method;
content:"metadata.svc"; http_uri;
content:"/DeviceMetadataService/GetDeviceMetadata|22 0d 0a|";
http_header; content:"User-Agent|3a
20|MICROSOFT_DEVICE_METADATA_RETRIEVAL_CLIENT|0d 0a|"; http_header;
fast_pattern:12,20; metadata: former_category INFO; classtype:misc-
activity; sid:2025275; rev:2; metadata:affected_product
Windows_XP_Vista_7_8_10_Server_32_64_Bit, attack_target
Client_Endpoint, deployment Perimeter, signature_severity Minor,
created_at 2018_01_31, performance_impact Low, updated_at
2018_01_31;)
```

There are many strings that it searches for in HTTP packets. Specifically:

```
MICROSOFT_DEVICE_METADATA_RETRIEVAL_CLIENT
```

You can find more about it here: https://learn.microsoft.com/en-us/windows-hardware/drivers/install/device-metadata-retrieval-client.

A student was once particularly worried about one of these, so I suggested following through with the analysis. They determined the IPs involved to be specific computers and that there was no periodicity with these alerts. In other words, they occur seemingly randomly, or better put, whenever someone inserted a USB stick into a computer. The student quickly realized that this was a policy matter. In a network with strict controls about the usage of USB sticks, this would be an important alert; however, for that customer at the time, it didn't matter.

I am providing this as an example to emphasize the fact that 99% of alerts that you will see in a network are false positives or benign. This is what makes network security analysis using IDS alerts difficult.

Summary

- IDS alerts are a critical part of security analysis.
- Not all alerts are created equal, and most are false positives, i.e., what they alert you about is probably not what the network activity was about (weird, I know).
- Familiarizing yourself with your network alerts is a good strategy to help you eliminate many of the false positives.
- Always respond to a new alert that has not been previously observed.
- Alerts change, so investigating new ones is a routine task for an analyst.

8 HUNTING FOR MALWARE

- Understand how malware operates in a network.
- Use tactics, techniques, and procedures (TTPs) to help you analyze traffic.
- Establish strategies that can help you stay up-to-date with the latest threats.

Overview

Armed with the ability to understand alerts, it is time to take the next step and actively hunt for malware using *Indicators of Compromise* (IOCs) and other publicly available information. This involves using *Open-Source Intelligence* (OSINT) and taking a proactive approach to identify worrisome signs in your network that go beyond alerts. In fact, alerts are just a component of threat hunting.

Hunting for threats

Threat hunting as an activity is straightforward to understand but difficult to develop as a habit. It is all about keeping up with the times, monitoring recent trends and the appearance of novel malware and other vulnerabilities, and then actively monitoring your networks for IOCs or the presence of vulnerabilities that can be exploited. It is proactive rather than reactive and can be summed up in the following steps:

- Check daily for active threats through reputable security sources.
- Understand the Threats, Tactics, Techniques, and Procedures (TTPs).
- Monitor your network for IOCs.

- Assess and patch vulnerabilities.
- Document and share findings.

This is meant to be a daily and iterative process, something you can do for fun while sipping your morning coffee or tea (whatever your preference—I won't judge).

Check for daily active threats

How do you check for daily active threats? Students often ask me this question and expect a single answer that works, but unfortunately, there are many options. I personally track alerts from blogs, social media, and even email newsletters. That said, there are some places that can help you get started.

Governments operate Computer Emergency Readiness Teams (CERTs). There is typically one per government, and they release news on the latest and greatest threats. For example, you can check out US-CERT (http://www.us-cert.gov/), which is technically part of the Cybersecurity & Infrastructure Security Agency (CISA). The UK has the National Cyber Security Centre (NCSC).

Beyond that, there are blogs such as Rapid7, Krebs on Security, and Threatpost. Security companies may also have blogs that inform individuals about recent threats, such as the one provided by Critical Insight (https://www.criticalinsight.com/blog).

There are also threat intelligence platforms such as AlienVault Open Threat Exchange (OTX). These may provide you with machine-readable intelligence that you can use in your IDS or analytics platform (more on that in a later chapter).

An example of such a report can be found here: https://www.cisa.gov/news-events/cybersecurity-advisories/aa22-108a. CISA provides information about TraderTraitor, a North Korean state-sponsored malware. There is background information and other technical details, some of which are not network-related. Often, these reports include detailed IOCs meant to be implemented by security groups as rules for IDS. Other information, however, can be used directly to hunt for worrisome events in your network.

Understanding TTPs

Understanding *Tactics, Techniques, and Procedures* (TTPs) is like getting into the mind of a hacker. TTPs are essentially the playbook that cyber attackers use to carry out their activities. Tactics are the big-picture goals, such as breaking into a network or stealing data. Techniques are the methods they use to achieve those goals, such as sending phishing emails or exploiting software vulnerabilities. Procedures are the step-by-step details of how they execute those techniques.

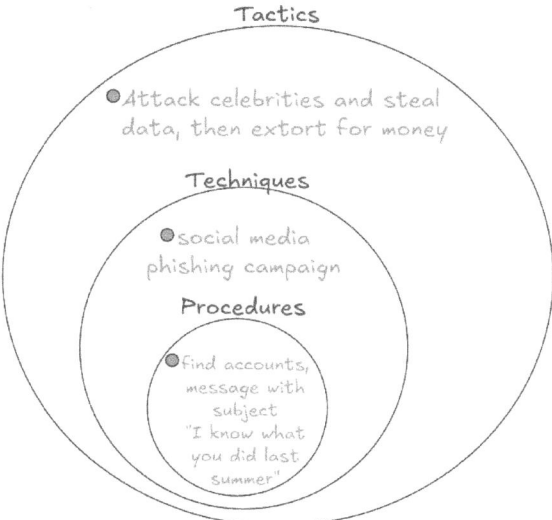

Regarding the example I used before (TraderTraitor), the article describes TTPs, which stand for Tactics, Techniques, and Procedures. It outlines tactics targeting system administrators to install malware through cryptocurrency applications. Techniques used include *spearphishing* (i.e., targeted email spam). The procedures are then detailed along with the code used for the malware and other IOCs. There is also a list of websites (i.e., domain names) that have either been created as part of this malicious campaign or are legitimate websites that have been compromised. The latter is not uncommon since many websites use off-the-shelf Content Management Systems (CMS) like Drupal and WordPress, which are often not maintained, leading to exploitable vulnerabilities such as the injection of new content into an existing legitimate website.

Monitor network

Once you know which IOCs you need to use to hunt for specific malware, you can investigate to see if you can find these in your network. Most likely, you won't, but you never know. After all, that is the purpose of malware hunting. Often, searching for IOCs involves looking for domain names or specific ports, but sometimes, depending on the data available, you may need to get creative. For example, how would you establish repeated login attempts or scans on a computer (also known as fumbling) using NetFlow? Well, NetFlow provides you with bytes sent to the server and bytes sent to the client, respectively. A connection attempt that fails is likely to either have bytes sent to the client be zero (i.e., no response from the server) or asymmetrical byte transfer such that the bytes sent to the client are much smaller than those sent to the server (e.g., in the event of login failures). The presence of multiple NetFlows, especially for TCP connections with low byte transfer, is another IOC of the aforementioned activity.

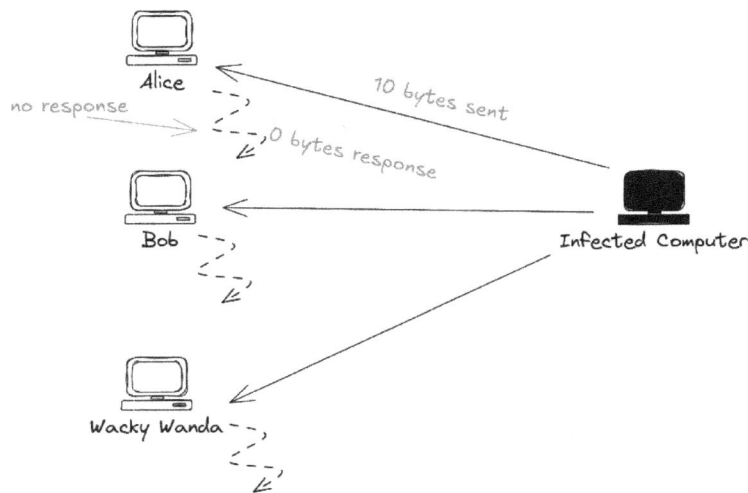

Assess and patch vulnerabilities.

Evaluating for vulnerabilities can be limiting when using just network data. Some vulnerabilities are detectable, but often the best approach is to determine if a vulnerable service is running on your network and ensure it is patched.

For example, if you are running a web server, check that the server is up to date along with the web framework. If you are using a CMS, make sure it's updated to the latest version. Procedures for this vary, and it would take a whole book to specify them. To simplify, if you have something running and connected to the network, make sure you have documented it, including its version. If it needs updating, identify the process through which it can be updated.

Running vulnerable software is also a practical decision depending on your risk appetite. There are hundreds of thousands of computers on the internet running vulnerable, old Windows versions, or current versions that are unpatched. It is a risk, and it should be mitigated, but it will depend on what you are protecting and the resources available to you. It is also true that just because something is connected to a network doesn't mean it is immediately exploitable by adversaries, even if a vulnerability exists.

Document findings

You will need to document your findings and potentially share them. An underappreciated aspect of threat hunting is knowledge management and the dissemination of findings. If you don't document that you've performed threat hunting, did you do it at all? Joking aside, documenting helps you further identify what's on your network and provides a reference to look back on. This can be done in the form of a report or by simply pasting information into a document. Many security companies today expect security personnel to use knowledge management systems (e.g., Wiki) and also produce reports to be presented to a wider audience, with some content redacted, of course.

Analyzing malicious patterns

Identifying malware follows a similar process to identifying attackers in your network. These attackers are also referred to as advanced persistent threats (APTs) since they are more advanced than the usual run-of-the-mill hackers and persist in your network much like malware does. To identify these threats, you have to follow in the footsteps of an attacker, which is consistent although the steps may occur out of order. For reference, these steps are called the Cyber Kill Chain and vary in literature. I am presenting below the most relevant ones to network security:

- Reconnaissance
- Delivery
- Exploitation
- Command and Control
- Actions and Pivot

Reconnaissance

There are two types of reconnaissance: passive and active. Passive reconnaissance is done using OSINT, where the attacker does not interact directly with your network. They investigate subnets owned by a company and any other publicly available information that could help them understand potential passwords and other privileged information. Active reconnaissance, on the other hand, employs various means to extract additional information that is not publicly available, such as open ports at the edge router or sending a phishing email to determine which email accounts are used. This activity, to some degree, is detectable through network data. For example, you can view all incoming connections from the internet to your local network in order to determine exposed ports.

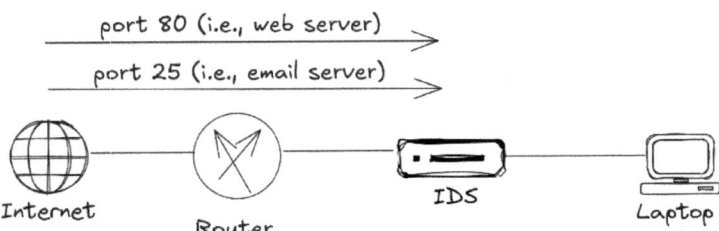

The good news is that if you have strict control over the edge router and your network, have disabled UPnP, and have not made use of port forwarding (i.e., exposing internal computer ports to the internet), then you have limited the likelihood of unexpected results. Another way to observe this type of activity is to look for spikes in email delivery. Spam is technically part of exploitation, as it often contains malware, but sometimes, with phishing campaigns, the intent is also to do reconnaissance. Monitoring for spikes on your email server, if you have one on your network, can help you determine this.

Delivery

This step is preceded by the weaponization step, which I have not included. Basically, the attacker will use the knowledge from the reconnaissance step to build an attack plan, and in the delivery step, they will execute that plan. For example, if they attempt a denial-of-service attack, you may notice spikes on your web server. You may also notice an outage on your web server if they are successful. If they attempt to run a series of exploits on your website, you are likely to see spikes in alerts. You will also see many short connections to the web server, likely from a single IP address.

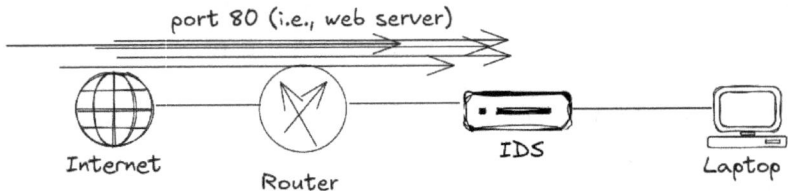

I should mention that if you observe the same activity but from various IP addresses, it may indicate a configuration issue or someone posting a wrong link about your website. In other words, expect some false positives.

Exploitation

Delivery and exploitation may occur as one step, but in the case of malware, what you receive in the delivery phase is often a loader that fetches the actual malware from somewhere online. This leaves network traces, such as fetching a file from an IP with a bad reputation.

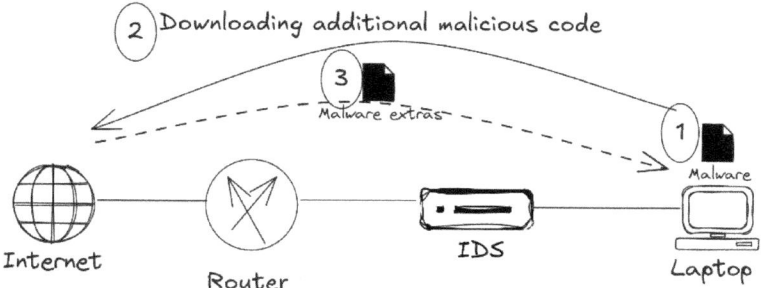

It may also create a bunch of noise in the form of alerts.

Command and Control

Right after the installation of malware is complete, it will attempt to open a backdoor in the system. However, this often requires port forwarding at the edge router or the use of UPnP to work. If the computer is on the DMZ (i.e., the edge of the network), the backdoor might be effective. Alternatively, if the computer is using a public IP address and no firewall is protecting it, the backdoor could also work.

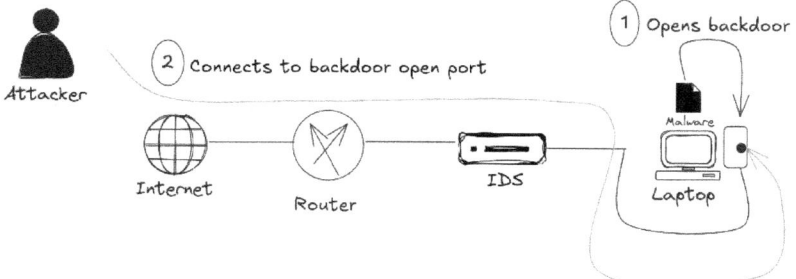

Technically a backdoor is just an open port, so, front door but I couldn't help myself in the diagram.

Anyway, in any other case where a backdoor is not possible, command and control communication where the malware communicates outward with the "mothership" is necessary. Where is the mothership? Somewhere outside a country's jurisdiction (or many countries', for that matter). The way that it often works is that the malware will contain the IP or IPs of the mothership, contain the domain names that in turn point to IPs, or use a Domain Generation Algorithm (DGA).

The last option is reserved for more advanced malware. Since IANA (the organization responsible for IPs, ports, and top-level domains) is quick about banning malicious domain names used by malware, the solution that attackers came up with was to build the malware in such a way that, depending on the time of day, it will attempt to reach a particular domain name. So, on 7/10/2024, it will attempt to reach xyazxrrew.com, but the next day it will be some other domain. The attacker understands this process, and all they have to do is register a domain name and point it to their IP address hosting their web server on that day. This way, even if the domain gets banned, it was just a daily. This is no different from the daily contact lenses that people wear and throw out at the end of the day.

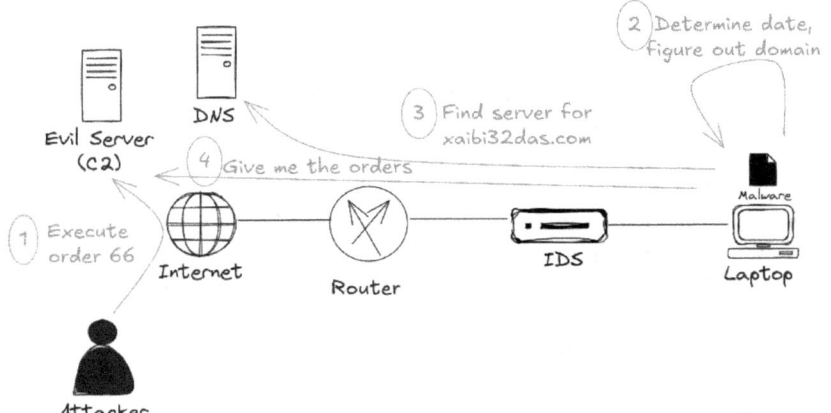

So, how do you detect command and control communications? DNS is a decent place to start. Look for odd or lengthy domain names or for domain names with a high Shannon entropy. This is a metric of the randomness of letters. The more unique letters you have in a domain name, the higher the entropy, since in most languages, letters typically repeat in words. Having said that, "google" is actually one of the domain names with relatively low entropy.

Z9q4rP7kH6xJ3vM2bYf9uN1.com
V6rL2wQ8pJ1xT0sK5mF4yB.org
R3z8nC7jK4tX0yP5wL9uQ.net

You can also look for unusual top-level domain names, such as ".top" or other uncommon domains for your location. For example, if you live in the US, then .sk domain names would be rare for your network. Beyond domain names, connections to IPs located in unusual places around the world or with a bad reputation would be useful IOCs. Some networks tend to connect regularly to odd places, so establish a baseline for your network, and then treat anything new as an unusual event to be investigated. C&C communications have a certain regularity. Since an attacker cannot directly command malware to perform actions, the malware must maintain regular communication with the command and control (C&C) server in case the attacker has tasks for it. Thus, frequent communication becomes another important IOC.

Actions and Pivot

When malware establishes itself, it may attempt to exfiltrate data or perform other actions. This can be detected using alerts or NetFlow. We've already discussed this in earlier chapters. It may also attempt to pivot. While inside a local network, pivoting involves port scanning and identifying other vulnerable systems (i.e., reconnaissance). This activity can be detected within the network. It also becomes much more dangerous since there are few systems (e.g., firewalls) to prevent the attacker from being successful. Refer to Chapter 9 for more information about internal threats.

Real-world example: Command and Control communications

One of the most exciting times for my students was when they discovered malware in one of the customer networks. It was a pretty wild find, and no alert caused this discovery. Instead, it was the fact that a student noticed communications to a strange location in the world that had never been observed before.

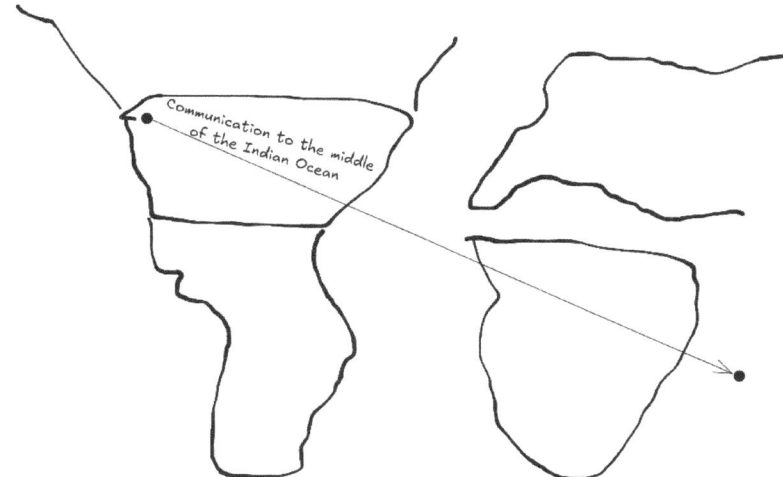

In the above map, I'm pointing to Mauritius, which has developed an

IT industry and is a popular choice for servers and VPNs. Don't be fooled by the location, as many C2 communications can also be domestic.

Back to my students. They determined the computers involved (a single local computer) and established that the communication was frequent and regular.

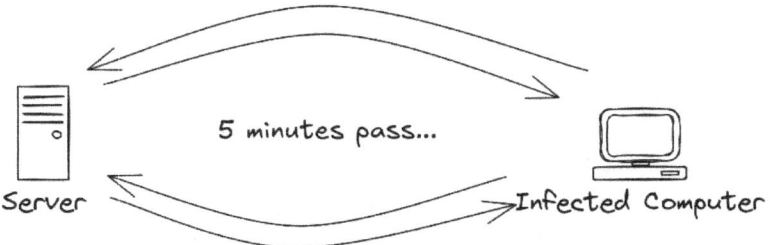

The communication was over HTTP, which is unusual but not extremely so, since many applications use HTTP (or HTTPS). It was the regularity and odd location of the IP that stood out. After using OSINT tools to determine the IP's reputation, we quickly confirmed that this was definitely an event that the customer needed to be notified about, and they were. The system was presumably nuked (i.e., disk wiped clean) because we stopped seeing that communication after a while.

Summary

- Establishing a habit of regularly staying informed about current network threats and malware is key to becoming effective at protecting your network.
- Tactics, techniques, and procedures are often provided by many key players in the security industry as a means to provide intelligence relating to threats. Use that information.
- Most malware has predictable steps and behaviors in networks, from probing to infiltrating and spreading.
- Pay extra attention to remote connections (inbound), outgoing connections to peculiar locations or those with a bad reputation, and domain names that appear randomly generated (high entropy).

9 RECOGNIZING THREATS FROM WITHIN

- Identify indicators of compromise for insider threats.
- Implement appropriate security measures to prevent the likelihood of an insider attack.
- Monitor for unusual activity on your darknet.

Overview

"I didn't see that coming." You'll hear this said about organizations and internal incidents, but the truer statement would be "I wasn't keeping an eye on things." The fact of the matter is that threats from within a network (also known as insider threats) not only exist, but they don't have to be an angry employee or family member. They can also be someone who managed to infiltrate your network and is now pivoting. No matter the reason, looking inward as opposed to outward is an important and very different step in network security analysis. The process is all about looking at IOCs that are often more generic than those for malware but fairly intuitive once you think about them for a second or two.

Finding indicators of inside threats

Let's start by getting into the mind of an attacker. You have just infiltrated a computer on a network, and you can use it to pivot to other computers. What do you think it looks like for that person? More often than not, they are seeing only the computer they have just infiltrated and nothing else.

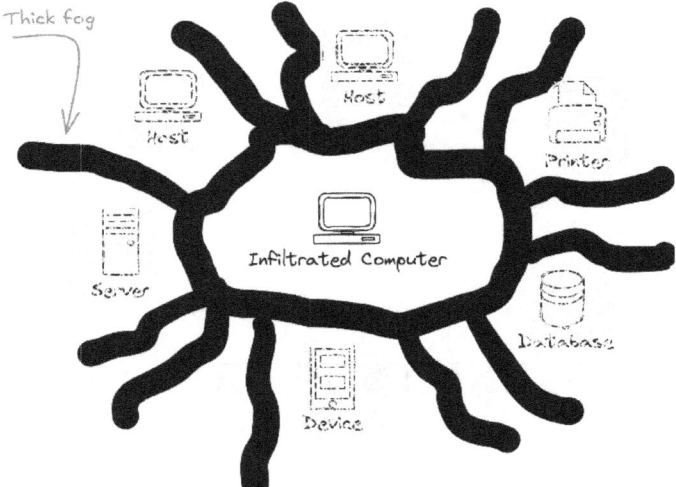

Since they may not know the physical space, they have no clue what's out there. To lift the fog, they will need to do reconnaissance. The passive method may involve looking at the Address Resolution Protocol (ARP) records in the system. ARP translates your IP address to a MAC address on networks so that a computer's packet can reach another computer or router. It is basically used for one-hop communication, as opposed to IP, which is for end-to-end communication (i.e., long-distance, computer-to-computer). The computer caches these records so that it doesn't constantly ask other computers on the network for their MAC addresses, and one can access the record assuming they have shell (or command prompt) access. This is not a complete record, but it will at least show the gateway and any other computers that the compromised computer has communicated with. Thus, the attacker's view changes.

ARP Request Broadcasted

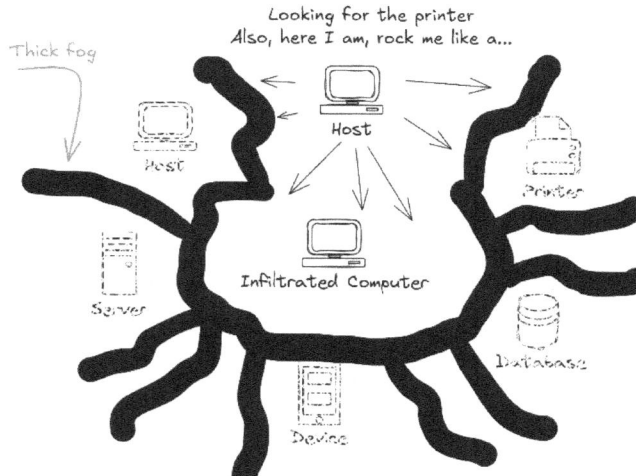

So far, there's no way to detect their activity, but they will likely move into active reconnaissance. For one, knowing IPs doesn't reveal what services they are running (i.e., what these computers are used for). Therefore, they will have to search for open ports in the existing IP addresses they know about. This is also referred to as a vertical scan.

Scanning incrementally for open ports

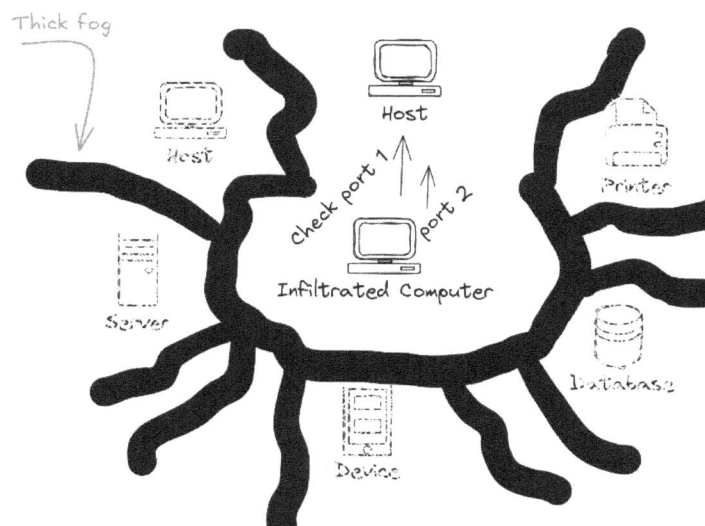

This can be done slowly and/or selectively. In other words, the attacker may choose to perform the scan over a period of a day or more. There are a total of 65,535 network ports available to computer systems, so sending a packet to each one can be noisy. Slowing down the scan helps to bury the noise. Not all these ports are useful, either. Many ports above 30,000 or 40,000 are used for the client side of a connection, allocated automatically by the operating system, and are called ephemeral ports. Servers very rarely listen for incoming packets on these ports. Most of the useful services like web servers, databases, and remote login servers are found on lower ports. Regardless, the first indicator of compromise (IOC) is to look for pairs of internal IP communications where multiple unique ports are used. NetFlows are great for this.

Destination IPs	Unique port count (over 1 hour)	
192.168.1.2	60	
192.168.1.3	3	
192.168.1.4	4	Possible targeted port scan

The attacker will also attempt to find other computers by scanning the network. By scanning, we mean sending network packets to different IP addresses. This can be done using ICMP (Internet Protocol's diagnostic protocol) ping, which sends arbitrary bytes to a computer and receives a reply. However, the "ping" utility (or echo protocol) can also be found in UDP and TCP variants and typically operates under port 7. Most systems are preconfigured to reply to ICMP, TCP, and UDP pings from computers or routers. An attacker will determine the current subnet by examining the infiltrated system's IP address (e.g., 192.168.0.1) and subnet mask (e.g., 255.255.255.0) and then conclude that they are in a /24 subnet. Based on this, they will scan every available IP in the subnet.

Scanning for present computers in 192.168.0.0/24

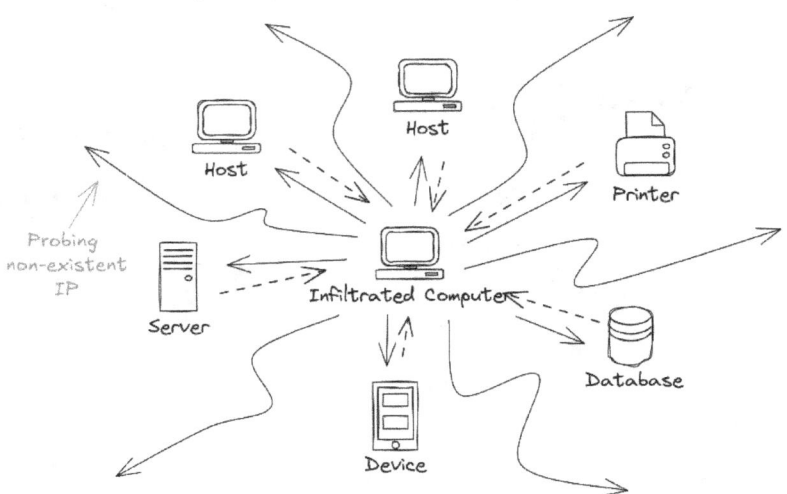

Notice the graph view and how it looks like a sea urchin. If you could graph the activity of an attacker from that computer, even if the scan was slow over a period of days, you would realize that someone is attempting to scan the network as more and more spikes are added to the infiltrated system.

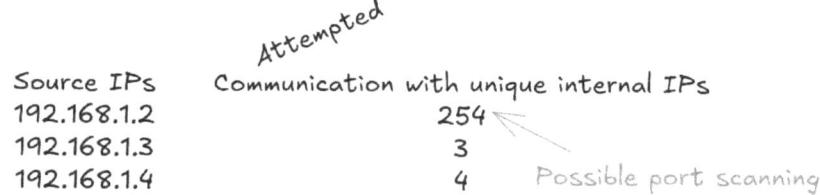

Give extra attention when a computer attempts to connect to an IP address that doesn't exist. The unused space in any subnet is referred to as the Darknet. The first time I saw this term mentioned in the context of security was in "Network Security Through Data Analysis" by Michael Collins. Not to be confused with "Dark Web," which refers to Tor networks, an area of internet inaccessible by regular routing software. Moving on, any activity toward those IPs should raise suspicion. After all, why would someone attempt to connect to a computer that doesn't exist?

Of course, making a graph to identify this activity is not realistic, so instead, all you need to do is look at the number of unique destination IP addresses based on the infiltrated (suspected) system's source IP address. The more packets it sends to various IP addresses in the local system, the more likely it is that a scan is underway. Notice that this approach is protocol-independent. The individual may send ICMP, TCP, or UDP packets to just about any port, and you will still see it. For example, an attacker may be looking for a database and send packets to a database port instead of the echo service (i.e., ping). That will still be visible in the network.

Once the attacker identifies the available computers within a subnet, they have a few choices:
- Test for vulnerabilities and attempt to exploit them.
- Start trying credentials to gain access (i.e., fumbling).

The first is likely to generate a lot of alerts. If that's the case, then looking for internal computer communication will show you a spike in alerts.

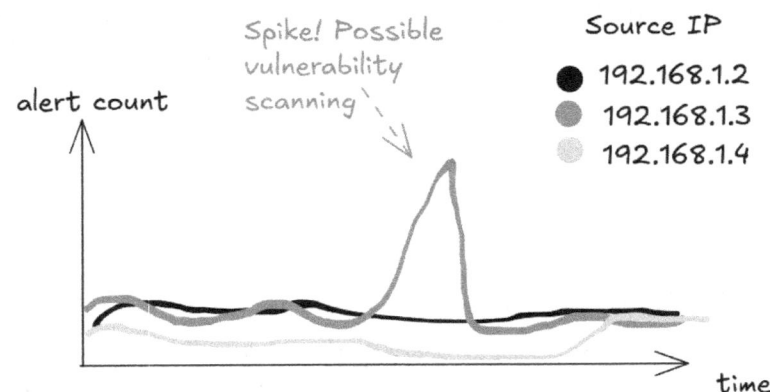

To be fair, this can also mean that something is misconfigured. Once, my students were getting repeated alerts about SMB scans due to a misconfiguration of a backup system that kept reconnecting instead of staying connected.

However, not all exploit attempts generate alerts. In that case, you'll need to look for unique repeat connections (not packets) from one internal computer to another. These may be attempts to exploit a system or an application that is misconfigured. Either way, it should be further investigated.

The final step for any attacker, should they be successful, is to execute their action plan and achieve their objective. For an insider threat, this is often data exfiltration, which we discussed in Chapter 6. Detecting this activity inside your network requires isolating data so that only internal communications are shown. Also, an attacker exfiltrating data is likely to eventually remove the data from the network, but they may do so at a slower rate to avoid detection.

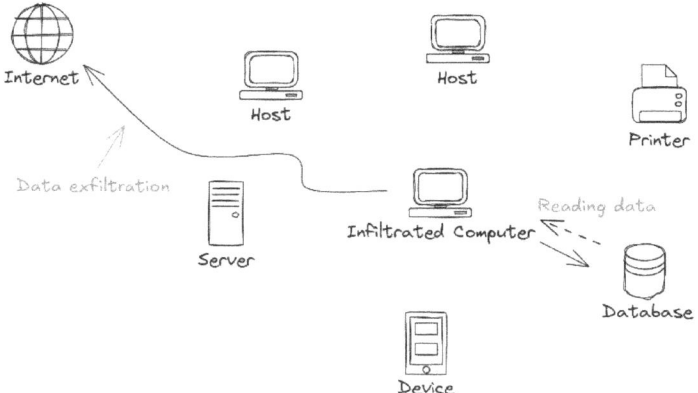

Scanning for present computers in 192.168.0.0/24

Strategies for mitigating insider threats

There are several strategies that can be implemented to help mitigate the risk of insider threats. These include policies and procedures, access controls, technical controls, and regulatory and legal compliance. Much of this is beyond the scope of network security. Therefore, I'll highlight the most important aspects in terms of network security: monitoring and incident response.

As the title suggests, mitigation is not prevention; hence, monitoring and incident response aim to limit the damage of a potential incident. For one, monitoring using IDS, performing audit trails, and implementing anomaly detection (more in Chapter 12) can assist in quickly detecting an insider threat. After all, knowing that something is happening in your network is the first step in deciding what to do about it.

Incident response involves deciding what to do about an event that you know is truly happening and is not a false positive. An interesting perspective on this is given in a TED Talk by David Teo (https://www.youtube.com/watch?v=Pf-JnQfAEew). In the talk, he describes a situation where someone on a network they were monitoring was running a torrent tracker server off of the company's network. This type of server enables torrent file exchange, and unlike merely downloading torrents, hosting a torrent tracker for the purpose of exchanging illegal files is considered more severe in the eyes of the law.

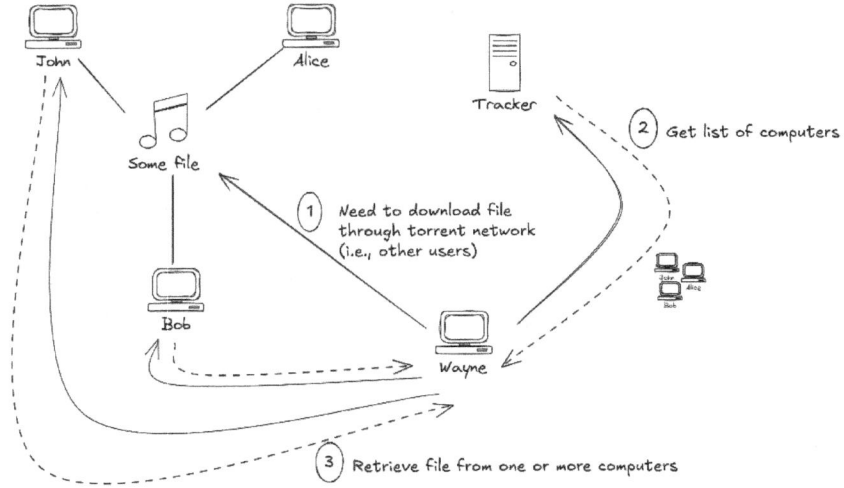

Detecting that such a tracker existed in their network was easy; they were informed about it by an external party. Finding who on the inside was hosting it was more difficult. It involved doing so discreetly (you can't just accuse people), doing it covertly (you don't want to tip off whoever is responsible), and doing it by the book (you need to collect evidence). They used network security monitoring to determine the computer involved in the tracking and then had to monitor the individual physically. Eventually, they determined that a USB drive was used to host the torrent tracker. Having collected all the data, they presented their findings to the company, which had to deal with the employee afterward.

You need to have an incident response plan in place and develop scenarios for what to do when something happens. This can also help you secure your network. For example, if you are running network-attached storage unencrypted, you may decide to encrypt it instead, taking a proactive approach.

Beyond that, you can run regular drills on your network. Pretend to be an insider threat and attack the network. Did you detect yourself? Or have someone else do it at an undetermined point in time. Red teams, as they are called, do just that. They attempt to break a system, evade detection, and the goal is for the defenders to detect them. It's like a simulated game.

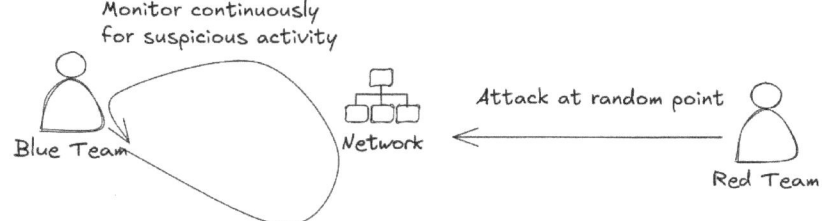

You need to also maintain a chain of custody for the data, but given that you are collecting and hopefully retaining your network data for some period of time, you are already one step in the right direction. By the way, cybersecurity insurance companies expect you to do so as well if you ever happen to purchase such insurance.

Real-world example: Too much chatter on the darknet

When my students monitor networks, they often have a hard time determining chatter on the darknet. The issue is not with the chatter part but with the darknet part. Most customers rarely provide us with adequate information about their network, so we have no clue what subnets they have (you cannot determine that easily through network data alone) or what types they are.

For example, a network will often have both a private and a public portion. To be clear, all IPs will be private (RFC1918, non-routable), but they will be used over Ethernet and WiFi. Some of the WiFi may be behind a password or, better yet, credentials, but some are public. So, while for Ethernet, we can easily look back for a month and see which IPs are not used in a subnet and speculate that this is part of the darknet, with public WiFi, we cannot do the same. Any user can just join, be given a random IP within a subnet, and then disappear.

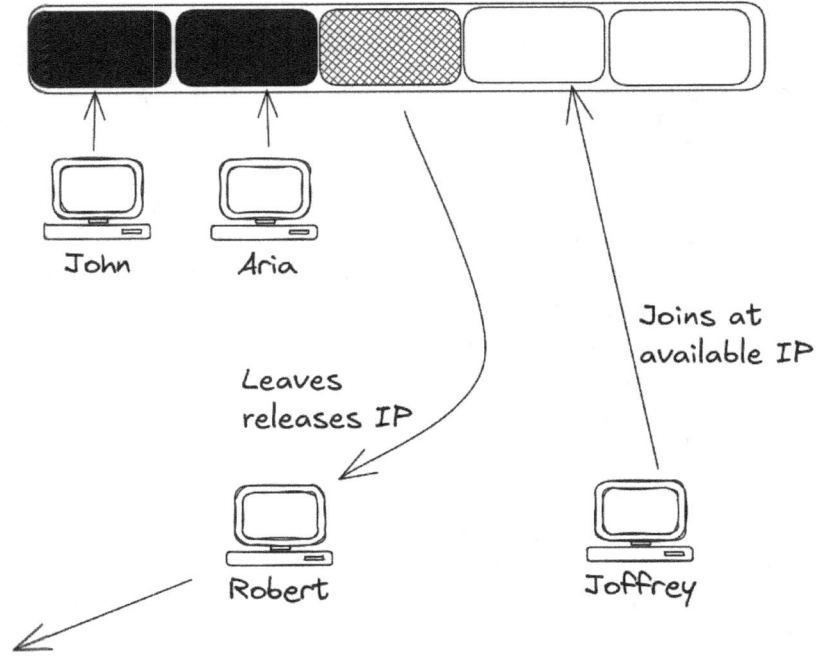

Scans on a public WiFi network may appear to be happening more frequently. It may indeed be the case, but we just don't know. It can also be challenging because there is often no easy recourse. Unless a user revisits the WiFi network, even if they are a malicious actor, it would be difficult to identify them and take action. Most monitored networks typically segment their private and public subnets so that one cannot access the other. However, they all converge on the edge router (also called the backbone of the network in this case), which is how we can see that traffic. Believe me when I say that people are concerned when this happens.

Real-world example: A worm amongst our mist

My students frequently see internal network scans. These can be a specialized type of malware that spreads through networks called a worm, or they could be a network administrator performing a diagnostic scan. Penetration testing (i.e., scanning for vulnerabilities) will also involve such a scan. How can you tell them apart? Well, you can't, to some degree, anyway.

Worms typically don't just give up but persist. Ransomware (i.e., a virus that encrypts your drive and asks for money) does the same. They will repeatedly try network IPs until successful. In contrast, penetration testing tools and system administrators usually perform scans at regular but spaced-out intervals, often once a week or more between each attempt.

So, I'm happy to report that all but one potential worm-like behavior my students have found was indeed not a worm. The one exception was a ransomware attack, which, by the time it happens, leaves little you can do to prevent the damage. You just have to hope that there are off-site (non-easily accessible) backups that are still intact.

Summary

- Detecting insider threats involves monitoring internal traffic and looking for indicators such as network scans.
- Scans can be detected by analyzing traffic with no response bytes or traffic directed to IP addresses that are otherwise unused.
- Insider threats with insider knowledge may intentionally target a particular system repeatedly. This is an indicator of compromise.
- Behaviors of fumbling should be tracked and investigated using the rinse-and-repeat method or similar approaches.

10 WORKING REMOTE OR ON THE CLOUD

- Learn how to enable and secure remote access to networks.
- Account for travel and remote work.
- Discover how the cloud fits into your network security strategy.

Overview

Networks have been evolving for quite some time, from early computers to the advent of portable devices such as laptops, to the Internet of Things (IoT) devices, and now remote devices. Post-pandemic, remote work has become the norm in many workplaces, extending well beyond IT. In fact, if you join just about any organization today, it would be surprising if a remote access option did not exist for their network. Some organizations with remote work options may provide you with more than one access point. Even in your home network, remote access can be an appealing option. Network security can be a challenge, but after discussing insider threats, monitoring remote access is not much different, as you will see.

Planning for remote access into a network

Let's start by discussing how to provide someone with remote access to a network. There are two major remote access options: remote login and remote network access. Remote login allows a user to access a computer remotely and operate on its desktop or shell environment. It is also part of a trend called zero trust, where individuals are limited to only the remote tasks and services needed to complete their work, and no more than that. Their credentials are verified at every step. The opposite paradigm is remote network access, often achieved via a *Virtual Private Network* (VPN). In this case, an individual has access to the remote network as if they were physically present.

Both options have security challenges. For example, ports need to be opened at the edge router to the outside world so that packets can be forwarded to internal computers running these services (i.e., port forwarding). For the internal computers providing these remote access services, additional security measures such as firewalls need to be implemented to restrict some of the most basic access that could compromise the network (e.g., blocking the IDENT service used to identify users over a network). Beyond that, these services need to be regularly patched, and credentials must be kept secure. Most organizations offering remote access today employ two-factor authentication (e.g., requiring both a password and a code sent to a phone) to allow someone to log in remotely.

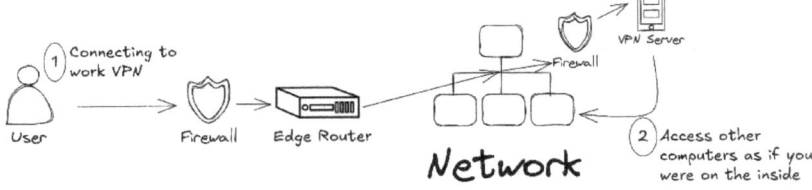

All this is to say, remote access isn't cheap, and it needs to be done correctly.

Traveling while working

In terms of network security, most network compromises related to remote access are not directly caused by the software itself. While it's possible for a hacker to discover and exploit a vulnerable version of a VPN service running on a network, this is relatively uncommon. Instead, most remote access compromises originate from the remote user's computer. Either the computer is compromised and the remote session is hijacked, or the remote login credentials are stolen, allowing the attacker to connect to the network using legitimate credentials. Once inside, the attacker behaves much like an insider threat, though without necessarily having insider knowledge.

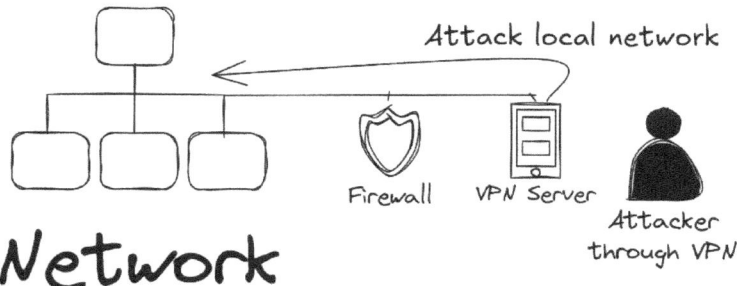

To prevent security risks, many companies provide employees with administratively locked laptops that have only the essential functions for the job. The logic is that if the laptop can only be used for work, it is less likely to cause harm. However, this doesn't necessarily stop employees from using their laptops in public places, such as a local café or favorite taco truck, and carelessly exposing sensitive information like credentials stored on a notepad. Other organizations may simply provide remote employees with VPN credentials, allowing them to use their own computers.

So, if you want to detect a malicious actor who has somehow obtained these credentials or used a compromised computer to pivot through a remote access service into your network, what do you do? Go back to the basics. If the server running the remote service in your network is exposed to the internet, why not treat it as if it is in your DMZ and monitor it accordingly—in other words, treat it as a non-trusted entity. For example, you can scrutinize the connections it receives and the origins of these connections.

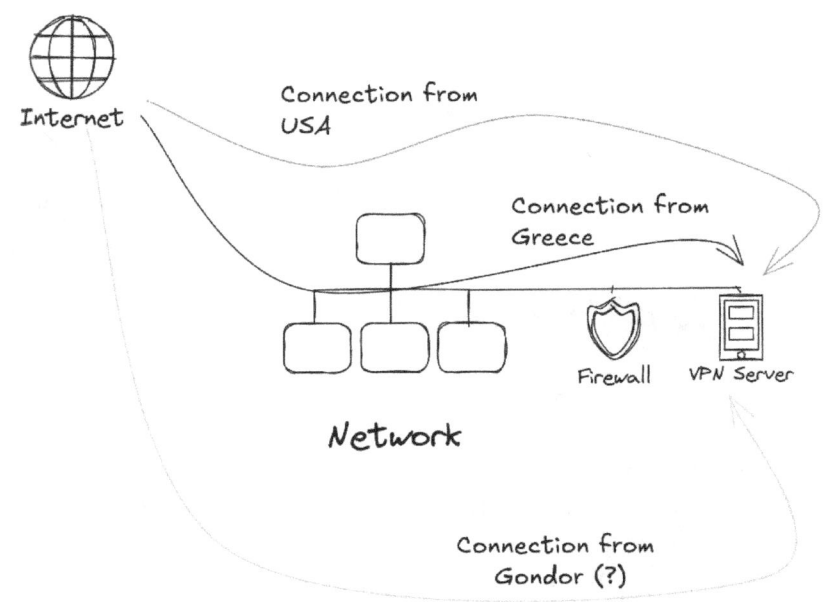

   Any places that appear to be peculiar, you may want to investigate. This is also the point where I typically hear from students to block country X and country Y. Well, yes, but the whole point of remote access is to allow people to access the network from remote locations. Banning goes against that, so if you plan to start banning entire country subnets (yes, you can find them and enter them in your firewall), at least put some thought into it and have a valid reason for doing so. You can also ban all and make exceptions, but adding to a security team's workload is not a wise choice.

   You can also check the number of attempted but failed connections to your VPN.

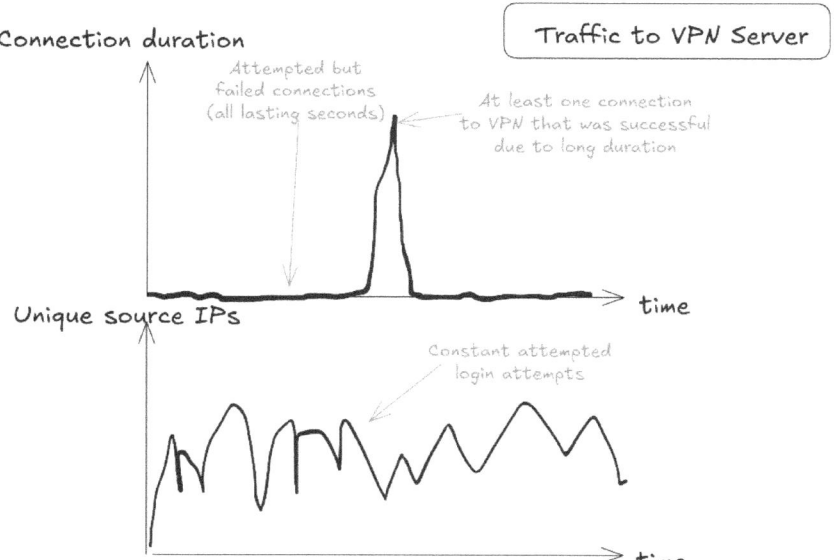

This may give you a valid reason to ban specific offending IPs. Typically, these are persistent and come from various VPNs around the world. These VPNs are privacy-protecting, and hackers often use them to mask their location. I can't count the number of times repeated login attempts to my VPN occurred from Mauritius or Seychelles. For small islands, they seem to produce a lot of hackers.

Viewing the duration of remote access sessions is also important. If you're using NetFlow, it's fairly easy to track, and by checking log data on who logged into your VPN, you can confirm if login times align with someone's travel plans or current location. For example, being connected from 2 AM to 6 AM from a US location when the company is in the US is unusual, whereas connecting from the UK to the US might be less odd, considering the time difference.

Finally, any sessions with large data transfers are suspect. You should raise an alarm as quickly as possible when file transfers exceed a certain size beyond the regular threshold. Anomaly detection can also help with this. More on that in Chapter 12.

Working with cloud services

Along with a changing world that embraces remote options, networks have been evolving for a while, shifting to cloud services. Need a database server? Amazon Web Services. Need a web server for your website? Google Cloud. Yes, I know that these services are not just called "cloud," but I'm just making a point. The fact of the matter is that, due to various factors, much of an organization's infrastructure has moved to the cloud (i.e., someone else's network).

These cloud networks typically apply network isolation to separate one network from another. That means your server on the cloud likely does not see any other computers. A compromise there is contained to just that server—or is it? Just because it's running on the cloud for cost-saving purposes doesn't mean the server doesn't need to be accessed or access your systems. For example, if you're using cloud backups, you're moving data to that server using some credentials. If the server is scheduled to run backups, the reverse can be true: it connects to your network and pulls data to back up using some credentials.

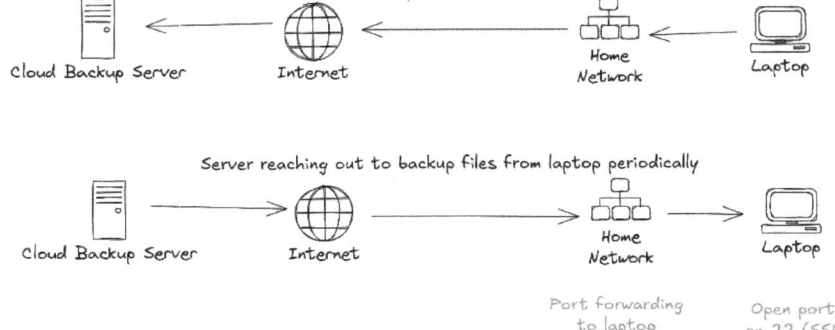

Which begs the question: If an IDS is placed in your network, who's monitoring that server? The answer can be a bit uncomfortable. There are logs in most of these services to determine what is happening to them, but placing an IDS there may be impossible or rather impractical. The practical advice is to treat that cloud server not as one of your own but as if it were someone else's. You will see it interacting with your network, and you will need to treat it as a foreign entity (i.e., not to be completely trusted). Keep an eye on the volumes exchanged, port connections, and any logs relating to who accesses it.

An extension of the above is that you can have multiple cloud servers for extra fun and connect them all in a Virtual Private Cloud (VPC). This is basically a full network in the cloud with all the bells and whistles of a real local network.

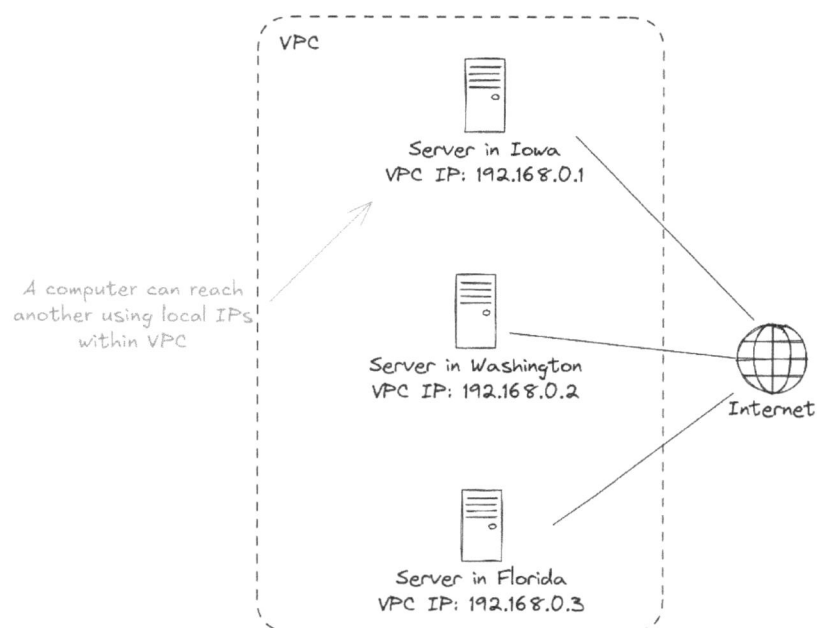

In this case, you have broad access to establish monitoring and data collection on that cloud network of yours. However, because many options are hidden behind convoluted menus, it can be a bit tedious to work with. You'll also be working against the current since historically there has been less effort for security monitoring on a VPC than on a LAN. The perception of security, ease of setup, and misconfigured tools can all lead to worse security outcomes for VPCs. But perhaps the largest reason is related to cost savings. The reason for moving to the cloud is saving a buck or two, and security monitoring costs the buck or two that you just saved. Thus, most people opt for old-school perimeter security (e.g., firewall) rather than more modern proactive approaches. Having said that, you are not without options. There are native monitoring tools and automated alerts provided by most cloud providers. They are far from perfect compared to what you can set up locally, but they can be adequate. For some providers, you may also be able to set up an IDS that sends data to your LAN. This can be expensive, but if full packet captures are substituted for NetFlow, the cost is an order of magnitude less.

A final discussion related to the cloud needs to be made about *Identity Access Management* (IAM). Some of my security students end up in roles related to IAM nowadays. These roles are not as exciting as security analyst roles and probably get a lot less credit, but their role is critical. IAM encompasses managing an organization's credentials and processes for authentication, along with other advanced functions such as single sign-on (SSO). IAM professionals decide that John and Sally perform the same tasks, create a role for them (e.g., "Paper Pushers"), and then attach permissions to that role. John and Sally each receive their own credentials along with VPN access and other related resources. They also sign a document stating that they need to be careful with how they use these credentials. John and Sally skim it quickly and hit accept or simply hit accept right away.

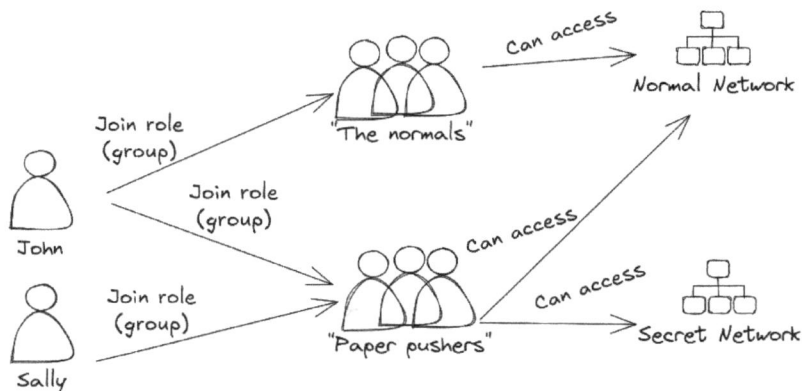

In regard to network security, you can request IAM administrators to apply the principle of least privilege to individuals. This can be achieved to varying levels of granularity depending on the network setup. For example, if you see too many IP addresses in the network accessing your database, contact the IAM administrator to discuss whether this access is necessary.

A more concerning trend is the indiscriminate sharing of IAM credentials and subsequent theft from employee computers. To understand this, let's do an exercise. Ask yourself: If your laptop were stolen today, what could the thief access? Windows credentials? Probably not, but it depends on the complexity of your password. Browser credentials? Probably yes, as they are often unencrypted or easily decryptable on your disk. An attacker could use these to infiltrate accounts and remote networks. Encrypting the disk is a step forward, and even better, encrypt using a keycode at the BIOS level.

To counter credential theft, organizations have aggressively implemented Multi-Factor Authentication (MFA). This typically involves using a phone code or authenticator app. However, even this is only as secure as the software facilitating MFA. Some MFA systems have a "don't ask me again" feature, which often leaves a cookie in the browser that associates the computer with an IP address. In other cases, it's enough for someone to declare the same IP address to the server, no cookie needed, to bypass MFA.

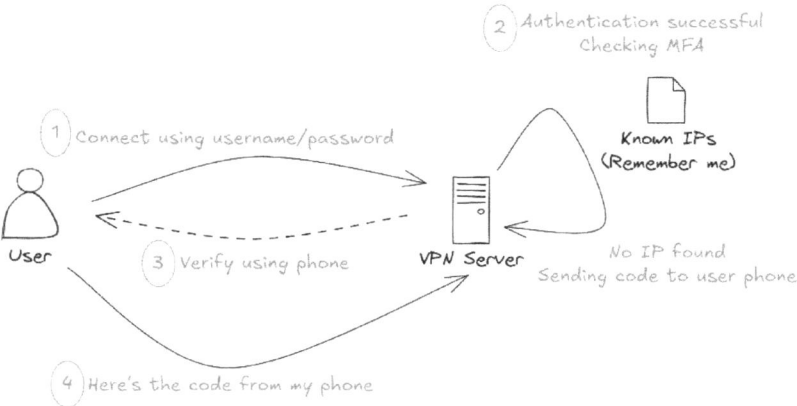

It unfortunately happened to my family, and MFA did nothing to protect us. So, what does all this have to do with network security and security analysis? Well, you need to be vigilant. Don't assume that because the IAM administrator is an ace and MFA is implemented, cloud or even remote access is safe. Keep looking for unusual IOCs. Your job is to be suspicious of everything. Keep collecting logs and running audits. Keep training your weakest links: humans. Finally, make a plan for how often credentials need to be rotated and what degree of difficulty they should have. I understand none of these directly relate to network security, but they affect network security.

Real-world example: Remote working and VPN

My students frequently encounter remote work sessions in many customer networks. Most sessions are typical, either US-based or within an internal network, and use OpenVPN (a type of VPN) or Remote Desktop Protocol (RDP). We can identify these by their ports, but because the protocol is UDP, it sometimes registers in unusual ways. For example, port 3389, the destination port for RDP, can sometimes appear as a source port in NetFlow data. This peculiar behavior is related to how UDP is measured using time windows and is often missed by students even when I highlight it to them. As a safer bet, look at the port: the lower one is likely the destination when it comes to UDP. TCP is safer because the way a session is tracked via NetFlow is different.

Aside from that, my students often need to determine the time and location of these sessions. The volume is also relevant, provided there is a historical precedent. If most past remote work sessions used 4 GB, then future sessions should be in that ballpark figure.

Here's the funny part: Recently, there has been a pattern where many alerts and other unusual behavior have been attributed to remote work. For example, a connection from England from a normal IP was deemed a remote work session, even though it used a VoIP port (not RDP or VPN) and was associated with an alert related to STUN binding. The point that students miss is that you can't put the cart before the horse. Yes, remote sessions exist, but you should build your story first using the steps discussed in chapter 6 (NetFlow). Remote work sessions don't just appear in a network; they come from specific IPs running remote work services such as RDP or VPN under specific ports.

Real-world example: Is it a backup?

Backups are common in most networks. Yes, even in your home network, there is likely a cloud backup to OneDrive or Dropbox. In customer networks, backups are typically directed towards the cloud. We can often detect them by looking at large volume transfers (depending on what is being transferred), but once my students detected one by accident. They started observing alerts for SSH scans (specifically, "ET SCAN Potential SSH Scan OUTBOUND"). They determined that their IP was on Amazon AWS (Amazon's cloud hosting service). This happened all of a sudden, and the alerts kept firing for a whole day. The signature has a suppression protocol for a few minutes, so the actual count of the scans or speed may have been higher than what we know. The fact that it was outbound means that someone from within the customer network decided to perform an SSH scan on some IP out on the internet. To be fair, "scan" is not the right word here. SSH runs on port 22, so you only need to "scan" once to know that the service is there. What the alert means is that there are SSH connections (TCP) that start and stop frequently. If they were malicious, it would mean that someone was trying random usernames and passwords on that SSH server. Suddenly, another local IP joined the party, raising alerts to the same destination IP on Amazon over port 22. Fun stuff, we thought, and also, weird enough to escalate. The customer identified that these were, in fact, backups happening to a cloud service provider and that there was a likely misconfiguration that kept forcing the SSH connections on and off while backing up.

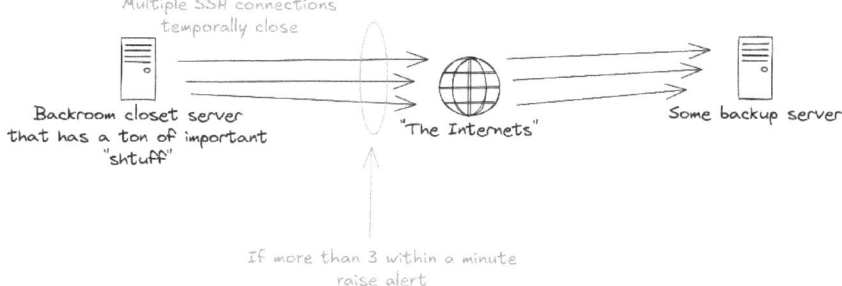

The whole thing was the software's fault, not something that the customer did. For many months, we kept seeing this alert whenever the backup would occur, although we have made a note to ignore the alerts now.

Summary

- Most networks will have a remote access point, such as a VPN server.
- Securing and monitoring this is paramount, as attackers can use it as a point of entry.
- Leaked credentials for individuals with access to this remote entry point are the most likely vulnerability.
- Placing a firewall and monitoring both inbound traffic to the VPN from the Internet and outbound traffic from the VPN to the rest of the local network is critical.
- Networks use cloud services for hosting various things (e.g., websites) and for backups. Identifying traffic to and from these services is important for security analysis.

11 POWERING UP YOUR SKILLS

- Learn how to use Generative AI to improve your understanding of security threats.
- Develop your skills further by using AI as a learning tool.
- Leverage AI to help you hunt for threats in your network.

Overview

Mark Antony, a prominent Roman general, deeply enamored with Cleopatra, Queen of Egypt, promised her a formidable alliance, envisioning an empire merging Roman strength with Egyptian wealth. Their grand promises and opulent displays of affection parallel the lofty claims of generative AI today. However, much like AI's frequent failures, Antony's assurances led to dire consequences. Their forces were defeated at the Battle of Actium in 31 BCE, and their dreams crumbled. Faced with capture, they chose to end their lives, a cautionary tale of ambitious promises falling disastrously short.

This chapter emphasizes the importance of keeping the reality of AI solutions to security grounded. It is easy to overpromise, which might even help you raise venture capital money, but be cautious when looking for silver bullets in security solutions. Many have tried, and I can safely say that they have all failed; breaches are still a frequent occurrence. However, a tool can be powerful if used properly and if its limitations are understood. That's what I want to convey with this chapter.

Using ChatGPT for network security

There are things that generative AI like ChatGPT can do and things

related to security. Here are the things it can do:
- Create or explain signatures and rules.
- Help you understand how a protocol works and which ports are frequently used.
- Assist with threat hunting.
- Help you write scripts and craft visualizations for your security dashboards.
- Assist in brainstorming ideas for security visualizations.

Notice that many of these include the word "help." This is intentional. While you could ask ChatGPT to solve problems for you, from experience, the solutions you get are far from ideal. The issue stems from how it really works. ChatGPT breaks a sentence into pieces (e.g., words or even smaller) and converts each into a vector. Think of this vector as a list of weights that were predetermined for each word during training. Then, it pushes these through thousands of layers where weights are adjusted in order to provide a final list that contains various words and probabilities. Then, it picks the highest probability as the next word to use for its sentence. This, in a simplified form, looks like this:

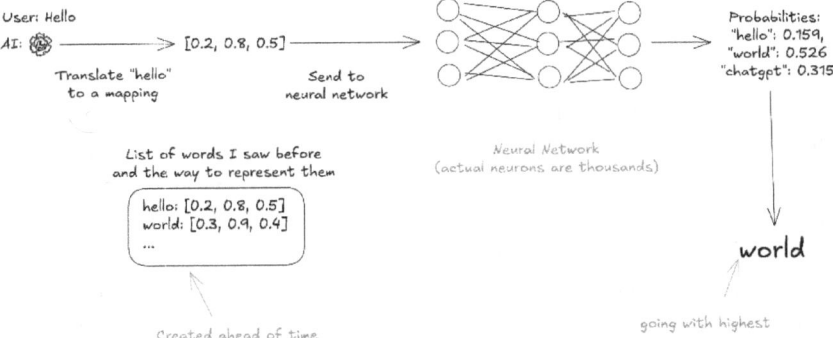

It is an oversimplistic explanation that I'm providing, but it is word-for-word prediction based on past words or portions of sentences, using thousands of parameters to predict the best next word. This can surprisingly create the illusion of intelligence. Or rather, some people claim that intelligence is just predicting words. Philosophy aside, the simplicity of generating results means that it can often produce erroneous or incomplete results. So, you need to be careful and always think of the output as something that can help you brainstorm rather than as if it is far superior to anything the human mind can produce.

The second limitation is a fault of ours rather than ChatGPT's. It will give you what you ask for, not necessarily what you want. For example, if you ask it the following: "Give me Kibana visualizations to detect data theft in my network." ChatGPT provided several visualization options for my network. However, in the absence of any knowledge about what data I have available, not everything was easily implementable. In my case, it suggested eight visualizations ranging from a heat map for abnormal user activity to a line chart for large file transfers. It did not provide a suggestion for DNS exfiltration, which would require a different approach to visualization and a different data source (DNS requests). So, my advice is to be as specific as possible when asking for something, and if you are not sure, then ask for various options and inquire again.

AI-Driven skill development

Another use for ChatGPT is as a learning tool to expand your horizons. Cybersecurity as a field is ever-changing. Today's spectacular new tool is yesterday's fad. Much of this book was written with that in mind, and the reason why most tools are in the companion repository is that they are bound to change. Yet, there is a lot of room for AI to help you develop the skills you need to excel in this ever-changing field. When I first started teaching students network security, I would have to tell them to read Suricata signature syntax and have them draft STIX 2. Most were not challenged by what they needed to do but by the how. AI can teach you syntax and can do it for you.

Another important aspect is to use it as an encyclopedia. This is especially true for determining TTPs for various threats or regulatory and other policy practices in respect to risk and compliance. For example, if you want to make your organization NIST 800 compliant, you can ask ChatGPT where to start and what points you should satisfy.

"I want to make my organization NIST800 compliant. What are the most critical parts that I need to have implemented or take into account in my network. Narrow down specific to network aspects."

The response that I received from ChatGPT includes things that appear to be optional or are phrased as such. For example:

"Network Segmentation: Implement network segmentation to isolate different parts of your network to limit access based on user roles and responsibilities."

Whenever this happens, you can go back and refine your initial request (i.e., by being more specific).

"I want to make my organization NIST800 compliant. What are the most critical parts that I need to have implemented or take into account in my network. Narrow down specific to network aspects that are required and not optional. Give them to me in a list 1, 2, 3."

The response was much more specific and focused. For example, part of the response included:

"*SC-1: Develop and document a system and communications protection policy and procedures.*

SC-7: Implement boundary protection, ensuring that external and internal network boundaries are protected."

You can then ask it specifically about each one of the items to identify the steps needed to satisfy these conditions. Finally, a caveat: training generative AI is costly and requires a lot of data, much of which must be curated to ensure that undesirable information is kept out of its training. This means that it is not always up to date, and its knowledge may lag anywhere from a few years to at least a few months.

Real-world example: Threat hunting

Threat hunting is a fun activity. It is a reason to hone your cybersecurity skills, and who knows, you may learn a thing or two or find something unexpected (but hopefully not). I have used this with my students, but I figured this time around I'll show you how to use ChatGPT to do the same.

"Give me the TOP 10 threats to networks that I need to be aware of in terms of recency and severity."

The response was too generic, so I needed to refine it. It took me a few tries, but here's what worked:

"Give me the TOP 10 threats with specific names (not categories) about networks that I need to be aware of in terms of recency and severity. For example, don't give me the category 'ransomware,' but give me the top specific ransomware."

Now I have a response:

Ryuk Ransomware: Known for targeting large organizations and demanding high ransom payments, Ryuk has been particularly severe in recent years.

TrickBot: A versatile banking trojan that has evolved into a modular malware platform, often used to deploy ransomware or steal financial information.

Maze Ransomware: Notorious for stealing data before encrypting it, Maze operators threaten to release sensitive information if the ransom is not paid.

SolarWinds Supply Chain Attack: Exploited vulnerabilities in SolarWinds software to distribute malware to numerous organizations, demonstrating the risk of supply chain attacks.

WannaCry Ransomware: Though older, WannaCry still poses a threat due to its ability to spread rapidly across networks using EternalBlue exploit.

Emotet: Initially a banking trojan, Emotet has evolved into a sophisticated malware distribution service, spreading other malware like TrickBot and ransomware.

Conti Ransomware: Known for targeting healthcare and industrial sectors, Conti uses sophisticated encryption methods and extortion tactics.

Log4Shell (Apache Log4j Vulnerability): A critical vulnerability in Apache Log4j that allows remote code execution, affecting a wide range of applications and services.

Phishing Attacks: Particularly sophisticated campaigns like Business Email Compromise (BEC) or targeted phishing attacks aimed at obtaining credentials or sensitive information.

Zero-Day Exploits: Unknown vulnerabilities exploited by attackers before the developers can patch them, posing significant risk due to the lack of available defense measures.

The response annoyingly includes still some generic items, but I'll let it slide. Let's pick Emotet.

"I have NSM and I collect Netflow, DNS and IDS alerts. Give me all IOCs for Emotet so that I can perform threat hunting. I want specifics so that I can use them directly on my analytics stack. Give me only those that I apply to the data I collect."

I had to expand and rewrite this several times to get the response I needed. Again, being more specific is better. Here's part of the response:

IP Addresses:
   Look for communications with known Emotet command and control (C2) servers:
      Example: 185.244.25.142
Domain Names:
   Check for DNS queries related to Emotet domains:
      Example: emotet[.]com
URLs:
   Identify URLs that Emotet-infected hosts attempt to access:
      Example: hxxp://example[.]com/emotet/update.exe

Now, I have something I can work with. Also, notice how nice it is not to provide the URL in HTTP format, as that would make it renderable by the browser, and I might have accidentally clicked it. That's a common security convention, but you can even ask about it, and it will tell you more. Anyway, on to threat hunting.

"Give me Kibana queries for each one of these."

Part of the response:

source.ip: "185.244.25.142"

dns.question.name: "emotet.com"

Notice that the queries are drafted based on some assumptions about the fields in our analytics stack. These may actually vary, and ChatGPT won't know about that. It is up to us to either refine them or find a

NetFlow record showing all the fields and copy-paste it so that ChatGPT can tell us which one to use.

Not sure what to use for source.ip. Here's my netflow record below. Can you tell me what field to use instead and refine the query for me.
[NETFLOW RECORD PASTED HERE]

The response was accurate for my setup: `flow.src_ip`. I even received an explanation about it, which I'm omitting here for brevity. Armed with all my queries, I can now search for Emotet signs on my network, and I'm happy to announce that there are none. Hurrah!

Summary

- Use AI as a tool to understand current and past threats.
- Ask it to explain concepts or syntax that you may not understand.
- Use it to speed up your work, especially with threat intelligence tasks or compliance.
- AI can also be used to speed up some tool configurations, such as building visualizations for network data.

12 BUILDING TOWARDS A PROACTIVE SECURE FUTURE

- Understand the process of responding to incidents.
- Learn about how to share and digest threat intelligence.
- Use some more advanced tools and techniques such as a SIEM and AI to enhance your security posture.

Overview

Network security and security analysis go far beyond the concepts covered in previous chapters. In fact, once you grasp the basics, there's a complex and ongoing process that involves communication, collaboration, and staying updated. AI also plays a significant role in enhancing this process. This chapter aims to provide a thorough overview of these aspects. The companion repository will demonstrate how to apply these concepts in practice.

Ticketing and escalation procedures

Typically, the job of network security—and by extension, monitoring—is not a solitary one, although I hear analysts like their solitude. Much like in other IT groups, tickets are used to organize people's work, identify issues or features to be developed, and bring them to a resolution or completion. For example, if you notice a critical malware alert, you can open a ticket in the system to convey your observation to other analysts. This may mean asking for help or simply documenting what you have observed.

Ticker #12345: Repeated connections to port 22

Connection have been consistently observed starting on 9/7/2024 at approximately 12am. See involved IPs below.

Src IP: 192.168.0.1
Dest IP: 192.168.0.100

Visit the link (https://stepstoreproduce/by8386232) to see further visualizations about this incident

Depending on the severity of the ticket and the respective escalation procedures in your organization, you may need to escalate the ticket to a Tier 2 security team or notify the customer, assuming the event is not a false positive.

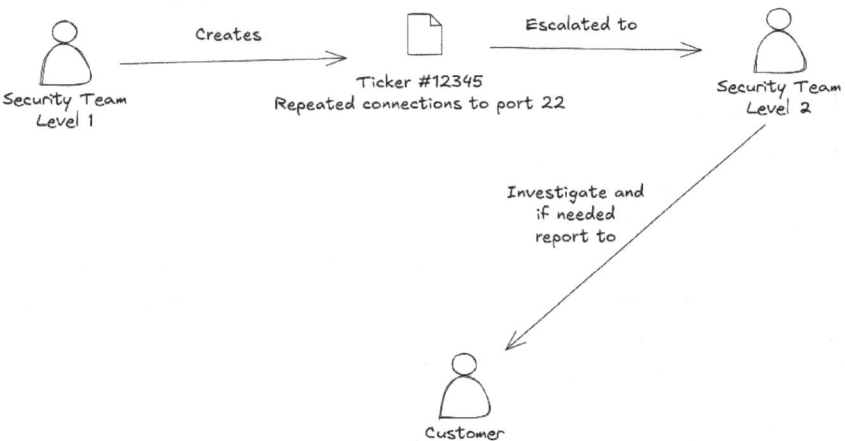

It may seem that what I describe is fairly trivial, but it's not. Numerous times, I see tickets that lack a good description or sufficient data documentation. Ambiguous ticket descriptions are frowned upon by other security personnel. After all, nobody wants to try and decipher what's on your mind. So, slow down and make sure to include in the ticket the most critical elements that you have identified.

Commenting on these tickets is also critical. If you are going to respond to a ticket, make sure that your response contributes to its resolution. It is tempting to want to be cordial and respond with an acknowledgment such as "great ticket," but that sadly just bloats the content in the ticket system and makes everyone's work more tedious. Save such comments for casual conversations, not the ticketing system.

If a ticket is ever escalated to a customer or the network team as something serious, there are a few critical steps to be mindful of. Communication becomes key, so don't be surprised if a Public Relations (PR) team contacts you or if you see social media posts related to an incident. These communications are often overly abstract and generic, aiming to control damage, but you may need to clarify some of the data. Documenting, data collection, and preparing presentations may also be on your horizon. Finally, you may not hear anything back from an escalation. Radio silence is also very normal since some internal security events are handled quietly by organizations or take a long time to be reported to the public (yes, even with regulations in place). It really depends on what you're dealing with.

Sharing and ingesting threat intelligence

The task of sharing and ingesting threat intelligence is a critical aspect of a security analyst's role. It is considered advanced because it often requires a team decision.

Let's start with ingesting. Security teams worldwide observe security events daily. Not all of these events are necessarily disclosable, but many are. If teams can notify others about their observations, the rest of the security community can be more effective. As a result, a more secure world benefits the team that shared the intelligence. This is essentially the reasoning behind sharing.

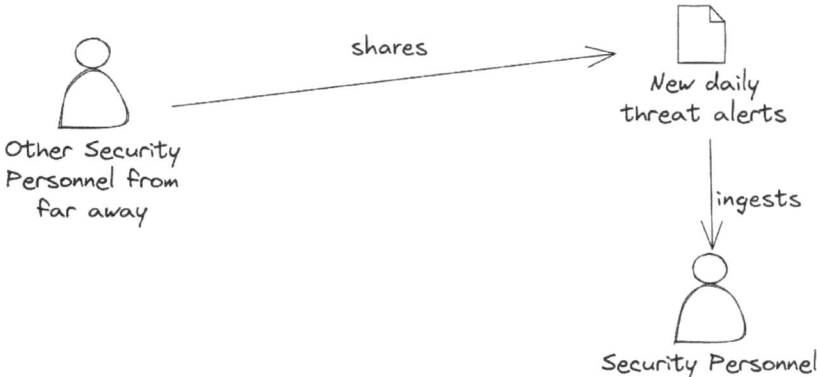

As to how, this is a bit more complicated. For the longest time, threat intelligence was shared using ad-hoc solutions, word of mouth, or social media. Some intelligence was shared in CERT reports, or antivirus and other security companies released what they saw in their blogs. This is chaotic and, worst of all, not machine-readable—or, put another way, not directly ingestible by machines.

This changed in recent years with the latest (and possibly greatest) solution coming in the form of the STIX2 framework, released by the Cybersecurity & Infrastructure Security Agency (CISA), which is part of the U.S. Department of Homeland Security (DHS). The framework contains a list of categories for different threat intelligence items, such as actors, TTPs (Tactics, Techniques, and Procedures), observed data, vulnerabilities, and indicators. These items can contain meta information related to their content and can be linked together. For example, for Emotet, one can provide the indicators along with the TTPs. This is all written in a format that is machine-readable (JSON). You can even use Notepad to write STIX2.

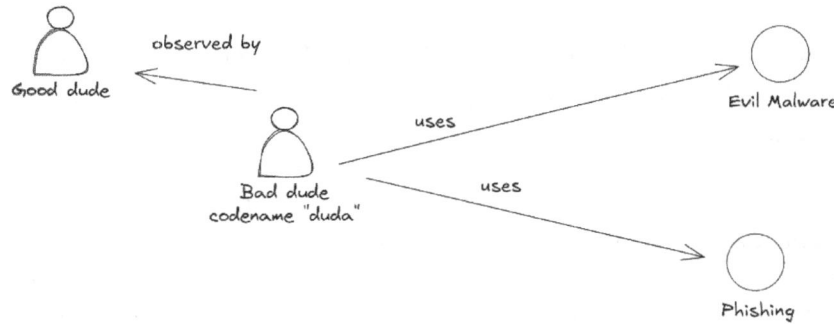

This tidbit of information can then be shared with other people. To facilitate easier transport of STIX2, a server-client architecture software for sharing was created called TAXII. With this, someone who wants to share intelligence can set up a TAXII server, and then anyone who wants to ingest intelligence can receive it using a TAXII client. Earlier versions of STIX2 provided generic indicators that had to be parsed through some other script to be implemented in IDS like Suricata. The newer version of STIX2 supports direct IDS queries. However, the true power is not in the likely signatures that STIX2 intelligence may contain but in the actual intelligence. Which hacker group is attacking whom and how? What is their attack chain? All of this is critical information that can help raise daily awareness about what is happening in the world.

Finally, sharing is the next step when a security team decides to start providing threat intelligence. From experience, maintaining such a threat feed can be a challenge. You need "signal" (i.e., data that produces enough events) and an experienced team that can reliably turn intelligence into STIX2. Syntax can also be a challenge, although ChatGPT can help with that.

Using Security Incident Event Management (SIEM)

A SIEM is the next level in event detection technology in security tools. Got a bunch of alerts from your IDS? Are you tired of trying to read them through visualizations? Or would you like to correlate them? A SIEM pulls not just from alerts but from multiple other data sources and tries to make sense of it all. This might sound like AI, but it's not. SIEMs have their own rule sets used to determine how one alert may relate to another or other incidents. It basically tries to determine whether there is an actual event happening based on multiple IOCs.

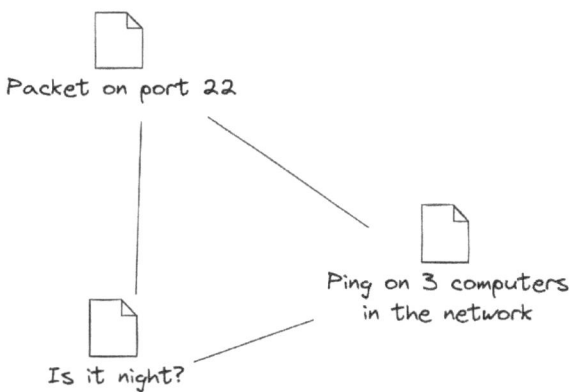
SIEM rule for detecting specific malware

What you would be doing manually, SIEM does for you. However, given the rigid rule set structure, SIEM is almost guaranteed to miss something. You can't know what's not in your rule set. Having said that, an asset is an asset.

Another major use for a SIEM is for compliance. For better or for worse, countries have passed laws to regulate various industries so that they meet a bare minimum set of security requirements. These regulations come with a set of rules that you need to follow. For example, don't leave unencrypted passwords in a database. A SIEM's rules can also help verify that you are meeting these requirements, which saves time documenting compliance.

So, after making the argument that you need a SIEM, how do you get one? It depends on your security analytics stack and the companion repository. I'm showing an example of a SIEM application. However, I would be remiss not to mention Sigma rules—basically a universal format for threat intelligence meant for SIEMs.

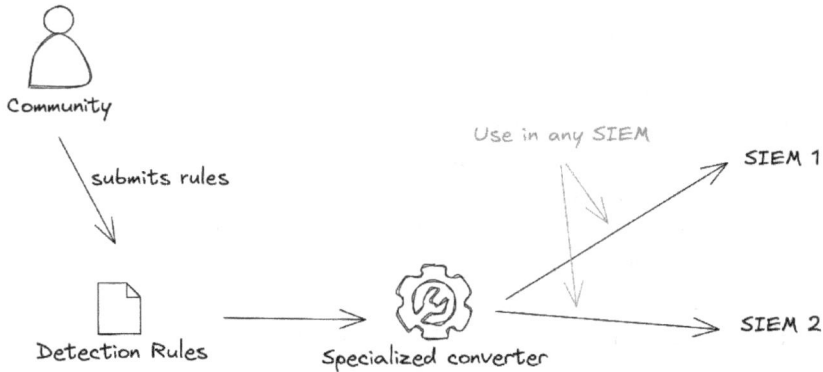

Extended Detection and Response (XDR) is considered by many to be the next step in SIEM evolution. XDR moves away from rules toward the use of advanced analytics and machine learning. There are also claims of more unified data collection, which can be challenged, as most SIEMs can achieve that too. The most significant change is that an XDR system aims to provide incident response. In other words, it can block networks or run scripts to respond to an event. This value is especially evident for malware such as ransomware. Shutting down a network may seem extreme, but given that most ransomware spreads to local computers via the network rapidly, response is more important than detection (i.e., by the time detection occurs, it is too late).

Boosting detection using AI

There is an ever-increasing attempt to employ more automated techniques to improve security event detection. Your mileage may vary depending on the tool you use. Effectiveness and the degree of effort required for setup may make these solutions prohibitively expensive to deploy, but it is still worth being aware of them. The companion repository demonstrates a few solutions in this advanced category. I'll concede that the term "AI" is a bit loaded here and caution you not to believe company ads that use the term. It is a buzzword; when you peel back the layers of how some of these tools work (when such information is disclosed), it is fairly simplistic. Instead, I'll highlight the most mainstream approach to AI security event detection.

Event Correlation

The first major step toward advanced detection is made by using alert (event) correlation. It is named this way because initially, it was about alerts and correlating them. If you come from a traditional statistical background, correlation may not make much sense in this context. Essentially, it means that if an alert happens and then another alert occurs, you should be notified about it. If you change the word "alert" to just about any event from different data sources, you have an extremely useful tool at your disposal. For example, if a query about a .top domain is observed and then any malware alert is raised by the IDS, that is an event you would want to be notified about. An IDS can somewhat perform this function but at tremendous cost because it would have to happen in real time. On the other hand, alert correlation on a SIEM occurs every few minutes, so the computational cost becomes more tolerable.

Anomaly Detection

The next big thing used in SIEMs and other advanced network security monitoring systems is anomaly detection. This is an umbrella term. Traditional security professionals recognize this through time-series analysis. Basically, you monitor a trend over time and look for an unexpected spike that does not match the trend. You can do this visually, but the automated approach aims to assist with this.

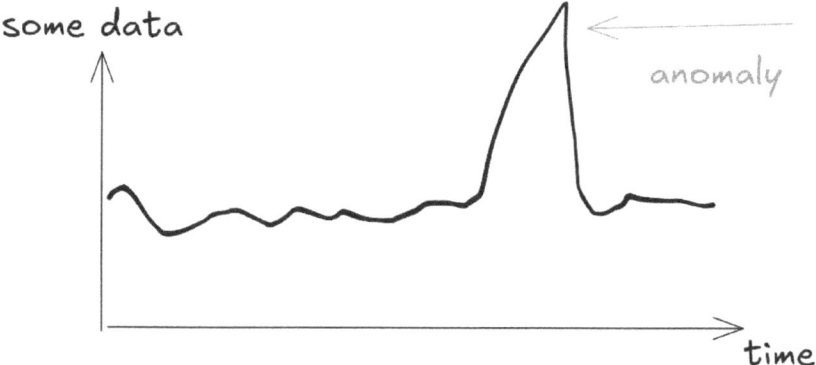

The key part is the feature that is selected to be monitored. The algorithm becomes the second most important choice. The simplest approach is using Holt's method. In the context of anomaly detection, Holt's method helps predict future values in data that have a clear trend or pattern over time. By comparing actual data to these predictions, we can spot unusual values that stand out as potential anomalies. If the actual data differs significantly from what Holt's method predicts, it might indicate something unusual or unexpected is happening. ARIMA is another more advanced model that adds the context of seasonality to the data and can thus make slightly more accurate predictions.

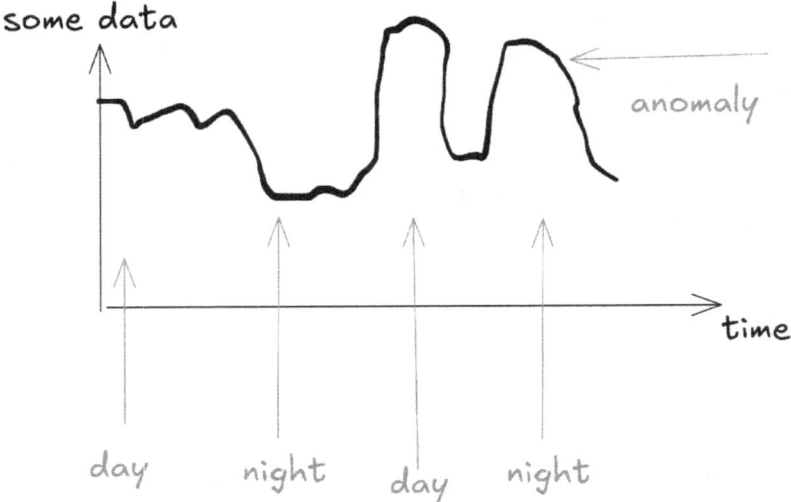

Again, the key to remember here is that, unlike the use of such models in other contexts (e.g., predicting stock prices), we do not attempt to predict. Rather, we see if the prediction matches our reality. Simply put, we do not forecast; we still observe the current state of the network.

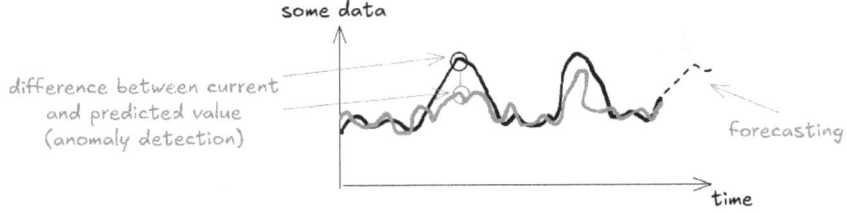

Other algorithms are also used for anomaly detection, such as *Random Cut Forest* (RCF). RCF detects anomalies by making random cuts in a dataset to isolate data points (similar to making cuts in a piece of paper). If a point is isolated quickly with fewer cuts, it is considered an anomaly. In network security, RCF can be used to detect unusual activity by analyzing patterns in network traffic data. For instance, most network traffic might involve regular data transfer between known devices. However, if an unusual spike in traffic occurs from an unfamiliar source or at an odd time, RCF will identify this quickly as an anomaly.

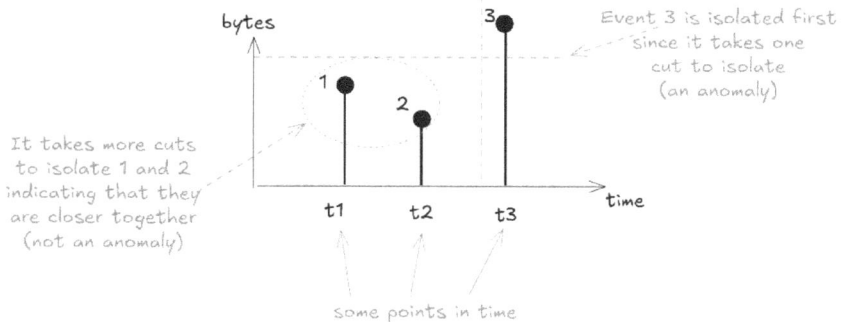

Finally, other machine learning and deep learning approaches exist, often requiring more extensive implementation and additional computational resources. Given that security often becomes secondary to the original cost of doing business, such implementations are less likely unless purchased and provided by a third-party company. Currently, commercial companies that provide SIEM or XDR software may offer machine learning options at a cost.

There is also a trend among security analysts utilizing programming languages (e.g., Python) to directly access data and build their own machine learning models. A word of caution regarding these models: they are susceptible to various attacks found in other machine learning and deep learning models. The most important one to be aware of is the "boiling frog" attack. It's actually a metaphor for slowly boiling a frog without it realizing it is being boiled (a gruesome image, I know). Anyway, assuming the attacker can guess your anomaly detection features, they can attempt to slowly increase the threshold by gradually increasing the activity for the respective feature used in anomaly detection. For example, if you want to detect spikes in byte transfers and there is a threshold at 10 MB over a minute, then a gradual increase that does not hit the threshold will raise the threshold higher.

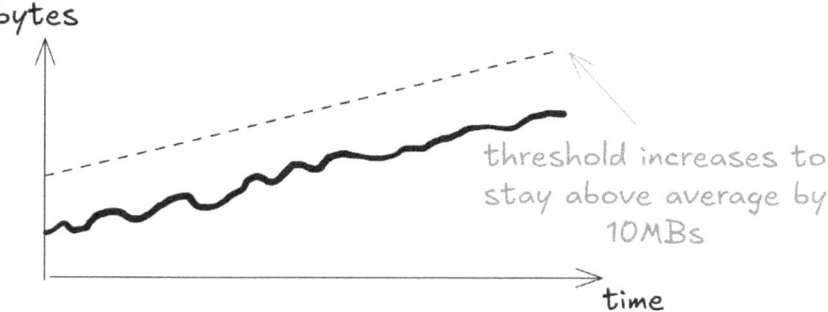

This is the case with many of the algorithms mentioned above. They all work on the concept of establishing a baseline, and anything that goes beyond this baseline will raise an alert. Raising the baseline becomes the trivial task of increasing the overall traffic without reaching the peak alert point, usually a certain percentage above the baseline. Models such as *Exponentially Weighted Moving Average* (EWMA) or *Long Short-Term Memory* (LSTM) Networks have better tolerance for boiling frog-type attacks, but they can, in turn, produce more false positives. In other words, because they are more sensitive to gradual changes, they are bound to alert for such changes more often. The big conclusion is that if you are looking for an AI silver bullet, it has not been invented yet and probably never will.

Summary

- Working as a team and organizing around events using tickets and other escalation procedures is a typical approach to security analysis in Security Operation Centers (SOCs).
- Sharing and ingesting intelligence on current threats through common security communication channels is essential.
- SIEMs are utilized in most SOCs to enhance the understanding of events and reduce false positives. XDR is added to improve or automate the response to incidents.
- Alert correlation and anomaly detection are two common tools used to help detect threats that singular alerts and other indicators of compromise might not reveal.

13 NEXT STEPS

- Understand the path ahead for network security.
- Discussion on careers and certifications.
- Additional learning resources.
- Celebrate! You've made to the end of the book!

Overview

There is so much more about network security than could possibly fit into a single book. It's just the nature of the field—everchanging and expansive. There is a lingering question whenever my classes wrap up: What next? In a similar manner, I wanted this book to provide people with a few directions. These are things that could not be reasonably covered in this book or what to look for.

Going beyond network security

The obvious direction one can take is moving from network security into the broader field of security, including cloud security, IAM, and even cryptography. From an academic standpoint, these are excellent choices, but you will soon discover that salaries can be quite variable. Ideally, you need to find a path with a good return on investment, and here's the kicker: it won't be a technical role. Yes, most of the high-paying jobs in security involve little to no hands-on coding (in whatever form that may be).

Instead, roles such as compliance, security assurance, risk management, auditor, and consultant are in the high-paying category but are also often considered fairly boring. Sorry to those in these categories, but checking boxes is hardly thought-provoking. Then again, I'm biased; I'll concede to that. Anyway, if you are looking to pursue these careers, the news is rather grim. Most paths leading to these roles start from positions in system administration, security administration, and the like. The path is an odd one: people with excellent tech skills often end up in higher-level positions where their skills stagnate, yet their contributions to the field do not. There is value in experienced security personnel who understand the threat landscape, which explains the higher pay. Of course, there are plenty of tech personnel who get paid well, too. I'm just discussing this proportionally.

So, my advice is to continue developing your technical skills. Plenty of people can write reports, but few can add value to these reports with their names and experience. The technical landscape, however, levels the differences. If you can perform a task, then you are an asset. So, where can you expand your skills?

Security engineering would be a great place to start. It pairs well with system administration experience, and you would be essentially setting up systems and ensuring they function seamlessly. From operating systems to microservices, containers, and virtualization, there is plenty to do.

Another area where you could expand your skills is in data science roles, specifically security-related roles such as designing new AI systems or refining existing methods. A big caveat here: this is a young field and carries a degree of risk, so do not put all your eggs in one basket.

The above two paths are fairly attainable and competence-based. Of course, becoming a good network security specialist or analyst is even better.

Certifications

You are likely to notice that there are several certifications used in the industry, many of which can be acquired either through an exam, while some require work experience. Of the ones that I suggest to people, CompTIA Network+, Security+, and CySA+ would be excellent candidates. Their themes are distinct and are recognized in the industry. There is also less bias with them compared to other certifications. Yes, they are sometimes seen as positives or negatives depending on the employer (yikes!). Another valuable certification to consider is the Certified Information Systems Security Professional (CISSP). This certification, offered by (ISC)², is globally recognized and highly regarded in the cybersecurity field. Unlike some entry-level certifications, the

CISSP requires candidates to have at least five years of work experience in the information security domain. This credential demonstrates a deep understanding of a wide range of security concepts and practices, making it a significant asset for professionals aiming for higher-level positions in security management and strategy. For those focusing on specialized areas within cybersecurity, the Offensive Security Certified Professional (OSCP) certification is worth mentioning. The OSCP, provided by Offensive Security, is highly respected for its practical, hands-on approach to penetration testing. Candidates must complete a rigorous 24-hour exam that tests their ability to conduct real-world attacks and vulnerability assessments. This certification is particularly valued by employers looking for experts in ethical hacking and penetration testing and showcases a candidate's ability to think critically and solve complex security challenges.

Further learning

In an ever-changing field, recommendations for what to read next can be a challenge. I would definitely recommend going through all the materials in the companion repository for practical experience with all the topics described in this book. It's time-consuming, but if you want to be seriously involved in network security, you need to acquire these skills. As for books, two hugely influential books for me are the following:
- Applied Network Security Monitoring by Chris Sanders and Jason Smith | Dec 19, 2013
- Network Security Through Data Analysis: From Data to Action by Michael Collins | Sep 8, 2017

I'll concede that both of these are dated; the tools presented can be remnants of a nostalgic and bygone era. However, the practice of security analysis presented in these remains everlasting. The core concepts of vulnerabilities, exploits, and threats have not changed for decades, nor are they likely to. So, if you are the reading type, this may be a good place to start.

Other than that, start following and watching popular podcasts on security or network security and make it a daily habit to stay informed about threats. You cannot be taught to have a security mindset, but you can organically evolve to develop one.

Summary

- Certifications are a must if you want a career in this field. Most

are fairly easy to pass with a bit of study, while others require work experience. Any certification is better than none.
- Seek additional resources, books, and other online material to enhance your skills and keep them up-to-date.
- Remember to have fun! This field can be a bit of a downer given the theme of constant threats and unhinged paranoia. Develop a sense of humor and entertain yourself once in a while.
- Also, thank you for reading this book and potentially going through the exercises in the companion repository. If you want to say something about this book, leave a review. Please share it online and with others you know through word of mouth. Your help is valuable and much appreciated.

AUTHOR'S NOTE

Thank you, dear readers, for taking the time to read Overnight Hercules for Network Security! Writing this book was a labor of love, and I poured my heart and soul into every page. Just like you, I am human with emotions and feelings, and I am grateful for your support and interest in my work.

As with any book, your feedback is invaluable. I'd love to know what you think! If you enjoyed this book, I invite you to leave a review and share your thoughts with other readers.

Thank you for joining me on this adventure, and I hope you enjoy the magic and wonder of the cybersecurity world.

ABOUT THE AUTHOR

Michail Tsikerdekis holds a Ph.D. in Computer Science and has dedicated over a decade to academia, contributing significantly through numerous academic papers and books, demonstrating a steadfast commitment to excellence. As an IEEE Senior Member and U.S. Fulbright Scholar he upholds high standards in his profession. Apart from his academic pursuits, Michail has delved into fiction writing, aspiring to advocate for diversity and inclusivity through his stories, envisioning a  world where everyone can pursue their dreams without limitations. Highlighting the importance of family, Michail values quality time spent with his loved ones. He enjoys engaging in outdoor adventures such as hiking and exploring, recognizing the significance of nature in promoting both physical well-being and family bonding. His aspiration is to instill a deep appreciation for the natural world in his children, fostering a love for the outdoors and creating cherished, enduring memories together.

www.ingramcontent.com/pod-product-compliance
Lightning Source LLC
LaVergne TN
LVHW012018060526
838201LV00061B/4357